Archibald Forbes

Glimpses Through the Cannon-Smoke

A series of sketches

Archibald Forbes

Glimpses Through the Cannon-Smoke
A series of sketches

ISBN/EAN: 9783337097271

Printed in Europe, USA, Canada, Australia, Japan

Cover: Foto ©ninafisch / pixelio.de

More available books at **www.hansebooks.com**

GLIMPSES THROUGH

THE

CANNON-SMOKE

A SERIES OF SKETCHES

BY

ARCHIBALD FORBES

BOSTON
JAMES R. OSGOOD AND COMPANY
1881

TO THE READER.

I have certain compunctions of conscience as to the title under which this little volume goes out to take its chance. It may be thought to have rather a lurid aspect of sensationalism: but there is nevertheless some fitness in it. I have spent the last decade almost wholly in campaigning, and have witnessed the cannon-smoke almost as often as I have seen the peaceful smoke from the domestic grate. My poor pen has been mostly engaged in efforts to describe military operations,— marches, battles, concentrations, and retreats. But intervals have occurred which I have humbly tried to utilize by work that is free at least from the fresh smell of burning powder; and it is some of that work which I have gathered up out of odd corners, and brought together in this little volume. I hope that work would have been better if it had not been in its nature so desultory; but there is this to be said for it, that there is a considerable variety in the subjects, and that some of the papers illustrate unfamiliar themes. Almost all, it should be said, are reprints; and I have to acknowledge my obligations to many people, for permission to reprint them.

LONDON, *June 1st*, 1880.

CONTENTS.

	PAGE
Matrimony among the Bomb-shells	1
An Evening Party among the Navvies	14
The Parade of the Commissionaires	26
Christmas Night in very Common Lodgings	36
How I "Saved France"	52
The Inverness Character Fair	66
Miss Priest's Bridecake	81
The Cawnpore of To-day	92
Christmas Presents by Post	108
On the Line of March	120
George Martell's Bundobust	128
Reverencing the Golden Feet	140
Christmas Day on a "Growler"	165
The Lucknow of To-day	177
Railway Lizz	206
A Hill Story	217

GLIMPSES
THROUGH THE CANNON-SMOKE.

MATRIMONY AMONG THE BOMB-SHELLS.

The interval between the declaration of the Franco-German war of 1870–1, and the "military promenade," at which the poor Prince Imperial received his "baptism of fire," was a pleasant lazy time at Saarbrück; to which pretty frontier town I had early betaken myself, in the anticipation — which proved well founded — that the tide of war would flow that way first. What a pity it is that all war cannot be like this early phase of it, of which I speak! It was playing at warfare, with just enough of the grim reality cropping up occasionally to give the zest which the reckless Frenchwoman declared was added to a pleasure by its being also a sin. The officers of the Hohenzollerns — our only infantry regiment in garrison — drank their beer placidly under the lime-tree in the market-place, as their men smoked drowsily lying among the straw, behind the stacked arms ready for use at a moment's notice. The infantry patrol skirted the frontier line every morning in the gray dawn, occasionally exchanging with little result a few shots with the French outposts on the Spicheren, or down in the valley bounded by the Schönecken wood. The Uhlans, their piebald lance-pennants fluttering in the wind, cantered leisurely round the crests of the little knolls which formed the vedette posts, despising mightily the straggling chassepot bullets which were pitched at them from time to time in a desultory way; but which, desultory as they were, now and then brought lance-pennant and its bearer to the ground — an occurrence invariably followed by a little spurt of lively hostility.

I had my quarters at the Rheinischer Hof, a right comfortable hotel on the St. Johann side of the Saar, where most of the Hohenzollern officers frequented the table-d'hôte, and where quaint little Max, the drollest imp of a waiter imaginable, and pretty Fräulein Sophie, the landlord's niece, did all that in them lay to contribute to the pleasantness and comfort of the house. Not a few pleasant evenings have I spent at the table of the long saloon, with the close-cropped red head of silent and genial Hauptmann von Krehl looming large over the great ice-pail with its *chevaux-de-frise* of long-necked Niersteiner bottles; the worthy Hauptmann supported by blythe Lieutenant von Klipphausen, ever ready with the "Wacht am Rhein;" quaint Dr. Diestelkamp, brimful of professional recollections of "six and sixty," and as ready to amputate your leg as to crack a joke or clink a glass; gay young Adjutant von Zülow — he who one day brought in from the foreposts a red-legged Frenchman a prisoner, across the pommel of his saddle; and many another — over most of whom the turf of the Spicheren or the brown earth of the Gravelotte plain now lies lightly.

But although the Rheinischer Hof associates itself in my mind with many memories, half-pleasant, half-sad, it was not the most accustomed haunt of the casuals in Saarbrück, including myself. Of the waifs and strays which the war had drifted down to the pretty frontier town, the great rendezvous was the Hotel Hagen, at the bend of the turn leading from the bridge up to the railway-station. The Hagen was a free-and-easy place compared with the Rheinischer, and among its inmates there was no one who dared call for the British brandy-and-water, who could sing a better song than manly George — type of the Briton at whom foreigners stare, who, ignorant of a word of the language, and wholly unprovided with any authorization save the passport headed "Granville George," and having not quite so much business at the seat of war as he might have at the bottom of a coal-mine, gravitates into danger with inevitable certainty, and tumbles through all manner of difficulties and bothers by reason of a serene good-humor that nothing can ruffle, and a cool resolution before which every obstacle fades away. Was there ever a more compositely polyglot cosmopolitan than poor young De Liefde — half Dutch, half German by birth, an Englishman by adoption, a Frenchman in temperament, speaking with equal fluency the language of all four countries, and an unconsidered trifle of some half-dozen European languages besides? Then there was the English student from Bonn, who had come down to the front accompanied by a terrible brute of a dog, vast, shaggy, self-willed, and dirty; an animal which, so to speak, owned his owner, and was so much the horror and disgust of everybody, that for his sake the company of his master — one of the pleasantest fellows alive — was the source of general apprehension. There was young Silberer, the many-sided and eccentric — an Austrian nobleman, a Vienna feuilletoniste and correspondent, a rowing man, a gourmand, ever thinking of his stomach, and yet prepared for all the roughness of the campaign — warm-hearted, passionate, narrow-minded, capable of sleeping for twenty-three out of the twenty-four hours, and the wearer of a Scotch cap. There was Küster, a German journalist, with an address somewhere in the Downham Road ; and Duff, a fellow of —— College, the strangest mixture of nervousness and cool courage I ever saw.

We were a kind of happy family at the Hagen; the tone of the coterie was that of the easiest intimacy, into which every new-comer slid quite naturally. Thus when, on the 31st of July, there was a somewhat sensational arrival, the stolid landlord had not turned the gas out in the empty *salle*, before everybody knew and sympathized with the errand of the strangers. The party consisted of a plump little girl of about eighteen, with a bonny round face and fine frank eyes ; her sister, who was some years older ; and a brother, the eldest of the three. They had come from Bohemia on rather a strange tryst. Little Minna Vogt had for her *Bräutigam* a young Feldwebel, of the second battalion of the Hohenzollerns, a native of Saarlouis. The battalion quartered there was under orders to join its first battalion at Saarbrück, and young Eckenstein had written to his betrothed to come and meet him there, that the marriage-knot might be tied before he should go on a campaign from which he might not return. The arrangement was certainly a charming one — we should have a wedding in the Hagen! There was no nonsense about our young Braut. She told me the little story at supper on the night of her arrival in the most matter-of-fact way possible, drank her two glasses of red wine, and went off serenely to bed, with a dainty lisping "Schlafen Sie wohl!"

While Minna was between the sheets in the pleasant chamber in the Hagen, her lover was lying in bivouac some fifteen miles away. In the afternoon of the next day his battalion approached Saarbrück, and bivouacked about two miles from the town. Of course we all went out to welcome it; some bearing peace-offerings of cigars, others the drink-offering of potent Schnapps. The Vogt family were left the sole inmates of the Hagen, delicacy preventing their accompanying us. The German journalist, however, had a commission to find out young Eckenstein, and tell him of the bliss that awaited him two short miles away. Right hearty fellows were the officers of the second battalion — from the grizzled Oberst down to the smooth-faced junior Lieutenant; and the men, who had been marching and bivouacking for a fortnight, looked as fresh as if they had not travelled five miles. Küster soon found the young Feldwebel; and the Hauptmann of his company, when he heard the state of the case, smiled a grim but kindly smile, and gave him leave for two days, with the proviso that, if any hostile action should be taken in the interval, he should rejoin the colors immediately, and without notice. "No fear of that!" was Eckenstein's reply, with a significant down-glance at his sword; and then, after a cheery "good-night" to the hardy bivouackers, we visitors started in triumph on our return to the Hagen, the young Feldwebel in our midst. It was good to see the unrestraint with which Minna — she of the apple face and frank eyes — threw herself round the neck of her betrothed, as she met him on the steps of the Hagen, and his modest manly blush, as he returned the embrace. Ye gods! didn't we make a night of it! Stolid Hagen came out of his shell for once, and swore Donner Wetter that he would give us a supper we should remember; and he kept his word. The good old pastor of the snow-white hair and withered cheeks — he who had been engaged to perform the ceremony of the morrow — we voted into the chair, whether he would or not; and on his right sat Minna and Eckenstein, their arms interlacing and whispering soft speeches which were not for our ears. The table was covered with bottles of Blume der Saar, the champagne peculiar of the Hagen; and the speed with which the full bottles were converted into "dead marines" was a caution to teetotallers. Then De Liefde the polyglot gave the health of the happy couple in a felicitous but composite speech, in which half-a-dozen languages were impartially intermixed, so that all might understand at least a portion. George, the jolly, insisted on leading off the honors with a truly British "three times three;" and that horrible dog of Hyndman's gave the time, like a beast as he was, with stentorian barkings. Then Minna and her sister retired, followed by Herr Pastor; and after a considerable number of more bottles of Blume der Saar had met their fate, we formed a procession, and escorted the happy Eckenstein to the Rheinischer Hof, where he was to sleep.

Next morning, by eleven, we had all re-assembled in

the second *salle* of the Hagen. In the great room the marriage-breakfast was laid out, and in the kitchen Hagen and his Frau were up to their eyes in mystic culinary operations. Minna looked like a rosebud in her pretty low-necked blue dress, and the pastor in his cassock helped to the diversity of color. We had done shaking hands, and were forming a circle prior to the commencement of the ceremony, when young Eckenstein started, and made three strides to the open window. His accustomed ear had caught a sound which none of us had heard. It was the sharp peremptory note of the drum beating the Alarm. As it came nearer, and could be no longer mistaken, the bright color went out of poor Minna's cheek, and she clung with a brave touching silence to her sister. In two minutes more, Eckenstein had his helmet on his head and his sword buckled on, and then he turned to say farewell to his girl ere he left her for the battle. The parting was silent and brief; but the faces of the two were more eloquent than words. Poor Minna sat down by the window, straining her eyes, as Eckenstein, running at speed, went his way to the rendezvous.

When I got up to the Bellevue, the French were streaming in overwhelming force down the slope of the Spicheren into the intervening valley. It was a beautiful sight; but I am not going to describe it here. Ere an hour was over, the shells and chassepot bullets were sweeping across the Exercise-Platz, and it was no longer a safe spot for a non-combatant like myself. Before I got back into the Hagen, after paying my bill at the Rheinischer and fetching away my knapsack, the French guns were on the Exercise-Platz. I heard for the first time the angry screech of the mitrailleuse, and saw the hailstorm of its bullets spattering on the pavement of the bridge. Somehow or other the whole of our little coterie had found their way into the Hagen; by a sort of common impulse, I imagine. The landlady was already in hysterics — the Vogt girls were pale, but plucky. Presently the shells began to fly. The Prussians had a gun or two on the railway esplanade above us, the fire of which the French began to return fiercely. Every shell that fell short tumbled in or about the Hagen; and a company of the Hohenzollerns was drawn up in the street in front of it, in trying to dislodge which, the French could not well miss the Hagen and the houses opposite. A shell burst in the back-yard, and the landlady fainted. Another came crashing in through a first-floor window, and, bursting, knocked several bedrooms into one. Then we thought it time to get the women down into the cellar, — rather a risky undertaking, since the door to it was in the back-yard. However we got them all down in safety, and came up into the second *salle* to watch the course of events. Hagen gave a fearful groan as a shell broke into the kitchen behind us, and, bursting in the centre of the stove, sent his *chefs-d'œuvre* of cookery sputtering in all directions. He gave a still deeper groan, as another shell crashed into the principal *salle* and knocked the long table, laid out as it was for the marriage-feast, into a chaos of splinters, tablecloth and knives and forks. The Restauration Küche on the other side was in flames, so was the stable of the hotel to the left rear. In this pleasing situation of affairs, George produced a pack of cards, and coolly proposed a game of whist. Küster, De Liefde, and Hyndman joined him; and the game proceeded amidst the crashing of the projectiles. Silberer and myself took counsel together, and agreed that the occupation of the town by the French was only a question of a few hours at latest. We were both correspondents; and although the French would do us no harm, our communications with our journals would inevitably be stopped — a serious contingency to contemplate at the beginning of a campaign. We both agreed that evacuation of the Hagen was imperative; — but then, how to get out? The only way was up the esplanade to the railway-station, and upon it the French shells were falling and bursting in numbers very trying to the nerves. However, there was nothing for it but to make a rush through the fire; and saying good-by to the whist-players, we sallied forth. To my disgust, I found that Silberer positively refused to make a rush of it. Although an Austrian, all his sympathies were Prussian, and he had the utmost contempt for the French. In his broken language his invariable appellation for them was "God-daammed Hundsöhne!" and he would not run before them at any price. I would have run right gladly at top-speed; but I didn't like to run when another man walked, and so he made me saunter at the rate of two miles an hour till we got under shelter. After a hot walk of several miles we reached the Hotel Till in the village of Duttweiler.

After all, the French, although they might have done so, did not occupy Saarbrück; and towards evening our friends came dropping into the Hotel Till, singly or in pairs. Küster and George brought the Vogts out in a wagon — it was surprisiug to see the coolness and composure of the girls. By nightfall we were all re-united, except one unfortunate fellow who had been slightly wounded, and whom a Saarbrück doctor had kindly received into his house. About nine o'clock, a company of the 2d Hohenzollern battalion marched into Duttweiler on its retreat from Saarbrück, and we were not long in learning that it was Eckenstein's company, and that he was all safe. The company was to halt in Duttweiler for the night; and when we heard this, George and Küster swore by Cupid and Hymen that, if it were possible anyhow, the interrupted marriage-ceremony should yet take place that evening. All entered into the spirit of the thing. Minna, like Barkis, was "willin'," and Eckenstein was eager. The Duttweiler pastor was routed out, and by eleven o'clock Minna Vogt had become Minna Eckenstein. Next morning, by seven o'clock, the young Feldwebel and his company were two miles forward on the road to the general rendezvous at Lebach. We were all up to see the start, and gave our young friend a hearty cheer, after George's monster flask had gone the round, and we had all shaken him by the hand and wished him well. In the course of the day the Vogts left for Saarlouis, to abide there with the kindred of Eckenstein till the war was over.

On the 6th of August came the Prussian recapture of Saarbrück and the desperate storm of the Spicheren. The 40th was the regiment to which was assigned the place of honor in the preliminary recapture of the Exercise-Platz height. Kameke rode up the winding road to the Bellevue; and then came the march across the broad valley, and, after much bloodshed, the final storm of the Spicheren, in which the 40th occupied about the left centre of the Prussian advance. Three times did the blue wave surge up the green steep, to be beaten back three times by the terrible gale of fire that roared down upon it from above. Yet a fourth time it clambered up again, and this time it lipped the brink and poured over the entrenchment at the top. But I am not describing the battle.

When it was over, or at least when it had drifted away across the farther plateau, I followed on in the broad wake of dying and dead which the advance had left. The familiar faces of the Hohenzollerns were all around me; but either still in death or writhing with the torture of wounds. About the centre of the valley lay the genial Hauptmann von Krehl—more silent than ever now; for a bullet had gone right through that red head of his, and he would never more quaff of the Neirsteiner; neither would Lieutenant von Klipphausen ever again stir the blood of the sons of the fatherland with the "Wacht am Rhein,"—he lay dead close by the first spur of the slope—what of him at least a bursting shell had left. On a little flat half-up sat quaint Dr. Diestelcamp, like Mark Tapley, jolly under difficulties; by his side lay a man who had bled to death, as the good doctor explained to me. While he had been applying the tourniquet, under a hot fire, his right arm had been broken; and before he could pull himself up and go to the rear, another bullet had found its billet in his thigh. There the little man sat, contentedly smoking till somebody would be good enough to come and take him away. Von Zülow too —he of the gay laugh and sprightly countenance—was on his back a little higher up, with a bullet through the chest. I heard the ominous sound of the escaping air, as I raised him to give him a drink from my flask.

What needs it to become diffuse as to the terrible sights that steep, and the plateau above it, presented on this beautiful summer evening? It was farther on the right, in ground more broken with gullies and ravines, that the 2d battalion of the Hohenzollerns had gone up; and I wandered along there amid the carnage, eking out the contents of my flask as far as I could; and when the wounded had exhausted the brandy in it, filling it up with water and still toiling on in a task that seemed endless. At last, in a sitting posture, his back against a hawthorn-tree in one of the grassy ravines, I saw one whom I thought I recognized. "Eckenstein!" I cried as I ran forward, — for the posture was so natural that I could not but think he was alive. Ah me! no answer came: — the gallant young Feldwebel was dead — shot through the throat. He had not been killed outright by the fatal bullet; the track was apparent by the blood on the grass, where he had crawled to the hawthorn-tree against which I found him. His head had fallen forward on his chest, and his right hand was pressed against his left breast. I saw something white in the hollow of the hand, and easily moved the arm, for he was yet warm: — it was the photograph of the little girl whom he had married but three short days before — the frank eyes looked up at me from the portrait with a merry unconsciousness; and the face of the photograph was spotted with the life-blood of the young soldier.

I sent the death-token to Saarlouis by post to the young widow. God knows whether she ever received it, for all the address I knew was Saarlouis. Eckenstein I saw buried with two officers in a soldier's grave under the hawthorn. Any one taking the ascent up the fourth ravine, Forbach-ward from the bluff of the Spicheren looking over to the Bellevue, may easily find it, about half-way up. It may be recognized by the wooden cross bearing the rude inscription: "Hier ruhen in Gott 2 Officiere, 1 Feldwebel, 40te Hohenzol. Fus. Regt."

AN EVENING PARTY AMONG THE NAVVIES.

It came in the way of my work some time ago to visit a colony of navvies engaged in the construction of the new line of railway then in course of being constructed between Settle and Carlisle. The headquarters of this scattered colony were on the slope of an outlying buttress of Ingleborough Hill, at the foot of which is a deep hole in the limestone, whence issues the headwaters of the Ribble. From some old legend of a suicide, this wild and savage place bears the curious name of Batty-wife-hole. Three or four hundred navvies were housed in the wooden huts, covered with black felting, that had been set down at haphazard on to the slope above the river-head, and there were various settlements bearing outlandish names bestowed upon them by the navvies themselves. Inkerman, Sebastopol, Belgravia, Jericho, Salt Lake City — all these could be reached with no greater exertion than half an hour's wade through the deep, treacherous oozy bog of which much of the moorland is composed. True, when reached, they were not much to look at, but they were racy of phases of that curious half-savage navvy life, which has in it so much that is interesting to the student of the by-tracks of human life.

While staying in Batty-wife-hole, I became acquainted with a family which I shall call Pollen. The father had been a navvy in his earlier days; but having saved a little money, had set up a tommy-shop, and was making money. His wife was a robust, powerful, purposeful dame, of immense energy, considerable surface-roughness, and real genuine kindliness of heart. During my stay, I was indebted to this burly navvy-woman for several good turns, in connection with which there could be no thought of self-interest. There was a married daughter who lived in a caravan at the gable of the parental hut, and there were two unmarried daughters, one an extremely pretty girl of about twenty, the other considerably younger.

Pollen had taken a letter for me down to Ingleton, and in the afternoon I looked in to see whether he had come back. His good lady reported his non-arrival, adding — "Afore we comed here, we were on the 'Surrey and Sussex;' and this morning, Betsy Smith, a lass as my daughter knowed there, comed here to see her mother, as is married on old Recks; and my girls, they be to have a holiday for to spend wi' their old friend. Well, I bid them tighten themselves up a bit, and tak' a basket, and go to the top of Ingleborough Hill, the three on 'em, for a day's 'scursion like; and when they'd come back, I'd have tea waitin' an' a cake, and I'd get in a bottle or two of wine, and we'd make a bit of a feast on't, you see, sir, for the lasses mayn't see one another no more in this here life." It seemed as if I had achieved the footing of a friend of the family; and Mrs. Pollen invited me, "if I would not think it beneath me," to look in and participate in the modest festivities of the evening. Beneath me! Why, it was the very thing I desired.

The navvy population of Batty-wife-hole do not keep fashionable hours. Half-past five was the hour named by Mrs. Pollen, and I was punctual. As I came up the road from the "Chum-hole," through Inkerman, to the mansion of the Pollens, the face of the swamp in the watery twilight was alive with navvies on their way home from work. They stalked carelessly through the most horrid clinging mire. What thews and sinews, what stately, stalwart forms, what breadth of shoulder and shapely development of muscle were displayed by these home-coming sons of toil! The navvy is a very rough diamond; but when you come to mix with him familiarly, and to understand him, you come to realize that he is a diamond. His character has never been more accurately delineated than in the words which I venture to quote, written by an engineer who knows him to his very marrow. "The English navvy has his bad points. Very bad points they are, no doubt, but, as a rule, they have all a common origin. The fountain of all, or almost all, the troubles of an English employer of this description of labor is the ale-can. But with these bad points there are many elements of the true pith and ring of the English character. Industry like that of the beehive; sturdy toil such as that which was commanded by the builders of the Pyramids, or the brick-building kings of Nineveh; firm fellowship and good feeling, evinced in subscriptions to sick funds and doctors' bills; clear-headed application of labor to produce a definite result; above all, a sense of the right that man and master alike have to fair play and honest dealing; all these virtues are to be found in the kit of the navvy. He is a man with whom there is some satisfaction in working, and a man as to whom you can attribute any failure in the attempt to elevate him into a position of permanent comfort and respectability not to any inherent infirmity of nature, but to want of early training, and to the potent influence of strong drink."

The "lasses" had got down from Ingleborough Hill, and were seated round the huge coal-fire in Mrs. Pollen's keeping-room. It was a state occasion; and the six navvies, who were lodgers, were relegated to their own sleeping apartment, where I found Mr. Pollen, slightly the fresher from his journey to Ingleton, having his hair cut by one of his lodgers prior to entering the sphere of gentility in the other room. Mrs. Pollen was painfully polite, and her notions of my capacities for rashers of bacon eaten along with buttered toast must have been based on her experience of navvies. The young ladies were at first slightly bashful, but Ingleborough air had given their appetite a beautiful fillip. Mr. Pollen was benignly jocose, with a slight tendency to hiccough. After tea, he entertained me with an historical account of Batty-wife-hole, from his first appearance in a van on its soil, exactly three years previous. Shortly afterwards, he said, " some chaps came down to make experimental borings, and they had to bide wi' us in the wan, for there were nowheres else to bide. All that winter there were ten of us living in that wan, and a tight fit it were, surely. Of a night I used to have to stand by it for half an hour with the bull's-eye as a guide to the men home-coming through the waste. Sometimes one would stick, and his mates would have to dig him out; there were two chain o' knee-deep water four times a day for the fellows atween their meat and their work.

"It were a winter! The snow lay on the backs of the hill-sheep for two months at a stretch, and many on 'em were frozen as hard as a chip. But we got over it somehow; and in the spring, Reeks and me built this cottage, and the works begun in fair earnest. There's been a good many deaths — what with accidents, low fevers, small-pox, and so on. I've buried three o' my own. I'm arter a sort the undertaker o' the place. You passed the little church down at Chapel-a-dale, near the head of the valley. Well, in the three years I've toted over a hundred of us down the hill to the little churchyard lying round the church. T'other day I had toted one poor fellow down — he were hale and hearty on Thursday, and on Tuesday he were dead o' erinsipalis; and I says to the clerk as how I thought I had toted well nigh on to a hundred down over the beck to Chapel-a-dale. He goes, and has a look at his books, and comes out, and says, says he: 'Joe, you've fetched to t' kirkyawd xackly a hundred and ten corps!' I knowed I warn't far out. They've had to add a piece on to t' churchyard, for it were chock-full. And there were one poor fellow I toted down the hill as don't lie in Chapel-a-dale. It were the first summer we were here, and a cutting had been opened outside the Dents-head end of the tunnel. Five men were in a heading as was being driven in along the track of the tunnel. There came on such a fearful thunderstorm as nobody hereabout ever saw the like afore or since. The end of the cutting was stopped up, and the water came tearing down the hillsides into it, and soon filled it like the lock of a canal. The chaps in the heading were caught afore they could get out; as the water rose, three swam into the cutting, and tried to scramble out. As the water rose, they got on a wagon that was in the heading, and tried to prop themselves up between some barrels that were on it. We could just see one, the tallest on the two — the face of him just above the water, and his hands held afore his mouth, to fend off the water that came lipping over him every now and then. He could get no higher for the head of the working, and it was horrible to see him. But we were tearing like mad at the bank of earth that was blocking the cutting, and at last we got a hole jumped through it, and then the water soon found its own vent, and emptied the cutting. The shorter of the two men in the heading were drownded, and his mouth stopped up wi' clay. He came from Kingscliffe in Northamptonsheer, hard by my own native place; and I got a coffin for the poor chap, and toted him down to Ingleton, and sent him home by the railway."

I don't know to what greater length Mr. Pollen's gossiping reminiscences might have extended, if they had not been interrupted by a tap at the door communicating with the room inhabited by the navvy lodgers. Sundry smothered and gasping squeakings of a fiddle had been audible lately from that apartment, the sounds being suggestive of the existence of an assertive and pertinacious violin, upon which the navvies were collectively sitting, sternly determined that while they lived, it should not violate the decorous quiet incumbent on lodgers whose respected host and hostess were entertaining visitors. The "lasses," I had noticed, were yawning a little after tea, as if the hill-air of Ingleborough had induced a somniferous tendency. As the tap was heard at the door, a glance of mutual intelligence and a smile of satisfaction passed round the younger ladies, and in truth Mrs. Pollen herself did not frown as she called, "Come in." Enter a stalwart navvy, whose powerful frame contrasted comically with his shamefaced countenance. He was blushing from ear to ear, yet there was a twinkle in the big black eye of the good-looking fellow that might speak of a consciousness he was not altogether taking a leap in the dark. He bore a message from the navvy brotherhood in the other room. He craved humbly of "Mother Pollen" that he and they should be admitted to participate in the festivities of the evening, whereunto they engaged to contribute by instrumental and vocal music, replenishment of the refreshments utterly regardless of cost, and good behavior. Pollen pronounced at once for their admission. Mrs. Pollen only stipulated for order; and the navvies trooped solemnly in, and seated themselves on the extreme edge of a form. Mrs. Pollen helped them to wine, of which all ceremoniously partook; and then the black-eyed navvy took Mrs. Pollen aside, an interview which resulted in the introduction of a pail of strong ale and a bottle of whisky. The navvies were a decided acquisition. First, the black-eyed navvy played a lively spring on his fiddle. I may remark, that he had imperceptibly edged off the form, and had dextrously taken up new ground between Miss Pollen and the lass from the "Surrey and Sussex." Then Tom Purgin sang *My Pretty Jane*. Mr. Purgin was a smart ruddy-faced young fellow with black curling hair, and the physical development of a Hercules. "Tom is the best man on this section," whispered Pollen to me. A dance followed —

something between a reel and an Irish jig — in which the black-eyed navvy immensely distinguished himself by playing and dancing at the same time; while the noise his big boots made in the double-shuffle was a Terpsichorean triumph that may be imagined, but cannot be described. The beer-pail was replenished, the ladies were radiant with good-humor and enjoyment, the navvies were making themselves as agreeable as possible, and the evening altogether was passing most hilariously.

The "Surrey and Sussex" lass was suddenly interrupted in the middle of a song by a loud knock at the outer door. Mrs. Pollen rose, and admitted a stranger, a big navvy in working-dress. This worthy had no card, but he "named himself" as the "Wellingborough Pincer." At a glance one could see that the "Wellingborough Pincer" was not quite so sober as he necessarily would have been if intoxicating beverages had never been invented. He was a new-comer at Batty-wife-hole, having only arrived that day; and being a Northamptonshire man, he had come to pay a visit to his "townie," as he had learned Mr. Pollen was. On Pollen the ties of "townieship" are binding; he hailed the "Wellingborough Pincer" with effusion; and that individual soon made himself extremely at home, resorting with marked freedom and frequency to the beer-can. Our own navvies were obviously chafing at the goings-on of the "Pincer," restraining themselves, however, for the sake of peace. His conduct was obviously leading to a shindy; and when he put his arm impudently round the waist of the "Surrey and Sussex" lass, nothing was more certain than that the affair, to quote Captain Marryat, "would end in a blow up." Mrs. Pollen had been absent for some time, engaged in serving some customers; but just at this crisis she came upon the scene, and comprehended its bearings with a quickness which may have been owing to intuition, but perhaps more to experience. To resolve, with Mrs. Pollen, was to act. In two strides she had the " Wellingborough Pincer " by the scruff of the neck, and was bundling him towards the door. He struggled a little, but Mrs. Pollen pinioned him with a vice-like grasp, and with a promptitude and dexterity which won my heartiest admiration, accomplished his ejection. I rather think she threw him out; anyhow, there was a sound as of a heavy body falling; and returning to the bosom of her family, she forbade any of " her men " from following the " Pincer " into the darkness whereunto she had relegated him. Harmony recommenced; the black-eyed navvy and I became confidential; and he told me how he had loved Miss Pollen for a considerable period, how they " had squared it together," and how he only wished that her father had another van in which they might take up housekeeping. In the midst of this interesting conversation, the " Wellingborough Pincer " re-appeared on the scene. Mrs. Pollen had not bolted the door, and he had entered, bent on apologizing all round, and expressing his heartfelt repentance for his conduct. It struck me at the time that the leading motive for the " Pincer's " apparent contrition was a keen anxiety to return to the neighborhood of the beer-pail; but he appeared sincere, and his expressions of sorrow were graciously accepted. He made the most of his time, and it was a caution to see what quantities of beer that man contrived to swallow. But he was an ill-conditioned dog in his cups. Without the slightest warning, he suddenly hit Tom Purgin in the eye. It was good to see that honest fellow's power of self-restraint. "It will keep till to-morrow," he said, with a pleasant smile, as he wiped some blood from the cut cheek-bone. This was Tom's own quarrel, and in his own quarrel he would not brawl in the presence of the women. But the blow had cut short the " Pincer's " stay under Mr. Pollen's roof. Again Mrs. Pollen was upon him ; again that determined and powerful female grappled him, dragged him across the floor, and sent him forth from the door. Enlightened by experience, she this time shot the bolt.

But this " Wellingborough Pincer " was an incorrigible and indomitable nuisance. He would not retire quietly after this his second ejection. He picked himself up, and commenced a persistent hammering on the doors and window shutters of the hut, accompanying this exercise with a voluble flow of execration of the people who were inside. With difficulty did Mrs. Pollen restrain her navvies from sallying out and inflicting condign punishment on the incorrigible "Pincer." But it was reserved for Pollen himself to vindicate the proud principle that an Englishman's house is his castle. Rising (with some little difficulty) from his seat, he oracularly pronounced the monosyllable "Joe!" At the word there emerged from under the table a powerfully built bulldog, whose broad chest, strong loins, muscular neck, and massive jaw, gave evidence of strength and purity of blood, as did the small red eye of unconquerable ferocity. Silently Pollen moved to the door with Joe at his heels. He threw it open just as the "Pincer" had commenced to rain on it a fresh shower of blows. "Here, Joe!" was all Pollen's reply to the volley of execrations that greeted him. There was a dull thud of a heavy fall, a gurgling noise, and at Pollen's word, "Come, Joe!" the dog reappeared, sententiously wagging his tail. The door was shut, and the "Wellingborough Pineer" demonstrated no more against it.

After a parting glass I withdrew from the festive scene, declining with thanks the offers of Tom Purgin and the black-eyed navvy to see me home. I examined the precincts carefully, out of what was perhaps a weak apprehension that the "Pincer" might be lying about somewhere, mangled, helpless, and perhaps indeed throttled. But that worthy was "gone and left not a wrack behind," and I sought my couch with equanimity. A day or two later Mr. Pollen called on me, and told me that he had received a summons at the instance of the "Wellingborough Pineer." Rather, indeed, there were two summonses, one for selling drink without a license, the other for setting a dog at that interesting gentleman. Mr. Pollen was game for litigation, and would hear of no compromise. The "Pineer" had called upon him that morning, and expressed his readiness to stay proceedings, on condition that the dog were shot, adding, that the doctor had assured him, were this not done, that his — the "Pineer's" — arm must inevitably be amputated. Mr. Pollen had requested him to go about his business, and was ready to face the magistrates in the serene consciousness of virtue.

I left the place before this *cause célèbre* was tried; but I subsequently heard its leading incidents. Mr. Pollen drove to Ingleton with his wife and his two wit-

nesses, Mr. Purgin and the black-eyed navvy. The
"Pincer" stated his case, and summoned a witness
who saw him worried by the dog. Then Mr. Pollen
arose and pleaded his own cause. He cited his wife to
prove that she sold no drink, but that the whole affair
was her "treat" in honor of the "Surrey and Sussex" lass. The magistrates asked particularly whether
it was in defence of his own premises that Pollen had
called in the assistance of the dog, and on being
assured that this was so, gave judgment against the
"Pincer" on both counts, condemning him also in
costs. On the way home, the Pollen conveyance,
which contained, in addition to the load it had brought
down, the "Pincer's" witness, was upset in the ditch,
owing, it was hinted, to the collective inebriety of the
passengers, but ultimately reached Batty-wife-hole,
and a triumphal entry was accorded to the Pollens.
The "Wellingborough Pincer" returned to work a
wiser if not a better man, but he was execrated by the
whole community for having imported legal proceedings into a colony where the policeman lived in a sort
of contemptuous toleration. Hints were uttered that
his career at Batty-wife-hole would be a short one.
The "Wellingborough Pincer" was last seen in the
neighborhood of a deep blind shaft, that had been
excavated to divert the water from the workings in the
tunnel. He may have suddenly migrated, but there
are not wanting those who darkly hint that an explora-
tion of the shaft would disclose the fact of his being in
the immediate vicinity of its bottom.

THE PARADE OF THE COMMISSIONAIRES.

On a Sunday morning in early June, just before the church bells begin to ring, there is wont to be held the annual general parade and inspection of the Corps of Commissionaires, on the enclosed grass plot by the margin of the ornamental water in St. James's Park. On the ground, and accompanying the Inspecting Officer on his tour through the opened ranks, there are always not a few veteran officers, glad by their presence on such an occasion to countenance and recognize their humbler comrades in arms in by-gone war-dramas enacted elsewhere than within hearing of the chimes of London Sunday bells. No scene could be imagined presenting a more practical confutation of the ignorant calumny that the British army is composed of the froth and the dregs of the British nation, and that there exists no *entente cordiale* between British soldiers and their officers. It is good to see how the face kindles of the veteran guardsman at the sight and the kindly greeting of Sir Charles Russell. Doubtless the honest private's thoughts go back to that misty morning on the slopes of Inkerman, when officer and private stood shoulder to shoulder in the fierce press, and there rang again in his ears the cheer with which the Guards greeted the act of valor by the performance of which the baronet won the Victoria Cross. There is a feeling deeper than a mere formality in the half-dozen words that pass between Sir William Codrington and the old soldier of the 7th Royal Fusiliers, to whom the gallant general showed the way up to the Russian front, through the shot-torn vineyards on the slopes of the Alma. When one feeble old ex-warrior is smitten suddenly on parade with a palsied faintness, it is on the yet stalwart arm of his old chief that he totters out of the ranks, and the twain do not part till the superior has exacted a pledge that his humble ex-subordinate shall call upon him on the morrow, with a view to medical advice and strengthening comforts.

Notwithstanding that in the true old martial spirit it shows what in the Service is known as a good front, it is not a very athletic or puissant cohort this, that stands on parade here on the grass, within hearing of the church bells. The grizzled old soldiers, sooth to say, look rather the worse for wear. There is a decided shortcoming among them of the proper complement of limbs, and one at least, in speaking of the battle-fields he had seen, might with truth echo the old soldier in Burns's "Jolly Beggars:"

And there I left for witness a leg and an arm.

They carry no weapons; to some may belong the knowledge only of the obsolete "Brown Bess" manual exercise; and not many have been so recently on active service as to have learnt the handling of the modern breechloader. On the whole a battered, fossil, maimed array of superannuated fighting men, scarcely fitted to shine in the new tactics of the "swarm-attack" by which the battles of the future are to be won or lost. But you cannot jibe at the worn old soldiers as "lean and slippered pantaloons." Look how truly, with what instinctive intuition, the dressing is taken up at the word of command; note how the old martial carriage comes back to the most dilapidated when the adjutant calls his command to "attention." Age and wounds have not quenched the fighting spirit of the old soldiers; there is not a man of them but would, did the need arise, "clatter on his stumps to the sound of the drum." There are few breasts in those ranks that are not decorated with medals. In very truth the parade is a record of British campaigns for the last thirty years. Among the thicket of medals on the bosom of this broken old light dragoon note the one bearing the legend, "Cabul, 1842," within the laurel wreath. Its wearer was a trooper in the famous "rescue" column. The skeletons of Elphinstone's hapless force littered the slopes of the Tezeen valley, up which the squadron in which he rode charged straight for the State tent of the splendid demon Akbar Khan. He rode behind Campbell at the battle of Punnier, and won there that star of silver and bronze which hangs from the famous "rainbow" ribbon. "Sutlej" is the legend on another of his medals, and he could recount to you the memorable story of Thackwell's cavalry operations against the Sikh field works, and how that division of seasoned horsemen reduced outpost duty to a methodical science. "Punjab" medals for Gough's campaign of 1848–9 are scattered up and down the ranks. The sword-cut athwart this wiry old trooper's cheek he got in the hot *mêlée* of Ramnuggur, where a certain Brigadier Colin Campbell, whom men knew afterwards as Lord Clyde, found it hard work to hold his own, and where the gallant Cureton — the "fair-

haired boy of the Peninsula "—fell at the head of his
light horsemen as they crashed into the heart of four
thousand Sikhs. His neighbor took part in the storm
of Mooltan, and saw stout, calm-pulsed Sergeant John
Bennet, of the 1st Bombay Fusiliers, plant the British
ensign on the crest of the breach, and quietly stand by
it there, supporting it in the tempest of shot and shell,
till the storming party had made that breach their own.
This old soldier of the 24th can tell you of the butchery of his regiment at Chillianwallah; how Brooks
went down between the Sikh guns, how Brigadier
Pennycuick was killed out to the front, and how his son,
a beardless ensign, maddened by the sight of the man-
gling of his father's body, rushed out and fought against
all comers over the corpse, till the lad fell dead on his
dead father; how on that terrible day the loss of the
24th was 13 officers killed, 10 wounded, and 497 men
killed and wounded; and how the issue of the bloody
combat might have been very different but for the display on the part of Colin Campbell, of " that steady
coolness and military decision for which he was so
remarkable." Scarcely a great show on a troop horse
would this bent and gnarled old 12th Lancer make to-
day, but he and his fellows rode right well on the day
for which he wears this " Cape " medal, with the blue
and orange ribbon, and the lion and mimosa bush on
the reverse. Because of its prickles the Boers call the
mimosa the " wait a bit " thorn, but there was no
thought of waiting a bit among the 12th Lancers at
the Berea, when they charged the savage Basutos and
captured their chief Moshesh. This one-armed veteran of the Royal Fusiliers was left lying wounded in
the Great Redoubt on the Russian slope of the Alma,

when the terrible fire of grape and musketry forced Codrington's brigade of the Light Division temporarily to give ground after it had struggled so valiantly up the rugged broken banks, and through the hailstorm of fire that swept through the vineyards. This still stalwart man was one of the 19 sergeants of the 33rd — the Duke of Wellington's own — who were either killed or wounded in defence of the colors on the same bloody but glorious day. A few files further down the rank stands an old 93rd man. The *ci-devant* Sutherland Highlander was one of that " thin red line " that disdained to form square when the Russian troopers rode in their masses at the kilted men on Balaclava day. He heard Colin Campbell's stern repressive rebuke — " Ninety-third, ninety-third, damn all that eagerness ! " when the hotter spirits of the regiment would fain have broken ranks, and met the Russians half way with the cold steel ; he saw the Scotch wife chastise the fugitive Turks with her tongue and her frying-pan. Speak to his tall, shaggy neighbor of the " bonny Jocks," and you will call up a flush of pleasure on the harsh-featured Scottish face ; for he was a trooper in the Greys on that selfsame Balaclava day when the avalanche of Russian horsemen, gliding off the face of the Sutherland men, thundered down upon the heavy brigade. He was among those who heard, and with sternly rapturous anticipation obeyed Scarlet's calm-pitched, far-sounding order, " Left wheel into line ! " He was among those who, when the trumpeters had sounded the charge, strove in vain by dint of spur to overtake the gallant old chief with the long white mustache as he rode foremost in the foe with the dashing Elliot and the burly Shegog on either hand of him; he was among those who, as they hewed and hacked their way through the press, heard, already from the further side of the *mêlée*, the stentorian adjuration of big Adjutant Miller, as, standing up in his stirrups, the burly Scot shouted, "Rally, rally on me, ye muckle ——!" Mightily knocked about has been this man with the empty sleeve, but he does not belie the familiar sobriquet of his old regiment; he was one of the "Diehards," a title well earned by the 57th on the bloody height of Albuera, and it was under their colors that he lost his arm on Inkerman morning. There is quite a little regiment of men who were wounded in the "trenches" or the Redan. There is no "19" now on the buttons of this scarred veteran, but the number was there when he followed Massey and Molesworth into the hell-abyss of the Redan on the day when so much good English blood was wasted. Shoulder to shoulder now, as oft of yore, stand two old soldiers of the Buffs, both of whom went down in the same assault; and an umwhile bugler of the Perthshire Greybreeks, "minds the day" well also by reason of the wound that has crippled him for life. As he stands on parade this calm Sabbath morning, that maimed man of the 60th Rifles can remember another and a very different Sabbath — the 10th of May, 1857, in Meerut — day and place of the first outburst of the Mutiny; a fell Sabbath of burning, slaughter, and dismay, of disregard of sex, age, and rank, of fierce brutality, and of nameless agony. His was one of the rifles whose fire, in the assault of Delhi, covered the desperate duty of blowing open the Cashmere Gate, performed with so methodical calmness by Home, Salkeld, and Burgess; and he was among his fellows of the 1st battalion who, when the hour had come for a rush to close quarters, followed Reid and Muter over the breastwork at the end of the serai of Kiesengunge. Proud, yet their pride dashed by sadness, must be the soldiering memories of this stout northman, erstwhile a front rank man in the old Ross-shire Buffs, a regiment ever true to its noble Celtic motto of *Cuidichn Rhi*. At Kooshab, in the short but brilliant Persian War, he fought in the same field whereon Malcomson earned the Victoria Cross by one of the most gallant acts for which that guerdon of valor ever has been accorded. He was in Mackenzie's company at Cawnpore when the Highlanders, stirred by the wild strains of the pibroch music, rushed upon the Nana's battery at the angle of the mango tope with the irresistible fury of one of their own mountain torrents in spate. And next day he was among those who, with drawn ghastly faces and seared eyes, looked into that fearful well, filled to the lip with the mangled corpses of British women and children. He was one of those who, standing by that well, pledged the oath administered by the bareheaded Ross-shire sergeant over the long, heavy tress of auburn hair which a demon's tulwar had severed from the head of an Englishwoman, that while strong arm and trusty steel lasted, to no living thing of the accursed race should quarter be accorded. And he was one of those who, having battled their way over the Charbagh Bridge, having threaded the bullet-torn path to the Kaiserbagh, and forced for themselves a passage up to the embrasures by the Bailey Guard Gate, melted from the stern fierceness of the fray when the siege-worn women and children in the Residency of Lucknow sobbed out upon their necks blessings for the deliverance. His rear rank man is an ex-Bengal Fusilier, wounded once at Sobraonwallah, again at Pegu, and a third time at Delhi. He will not be offended if you hail him as one of the "old Dirty-shirts;" for it was in honorable disregard of appearances, as they toiled night and day in the trenches of Delhi, that the regiment, which now in the Queen's service is numbered 101, gained the *sobriquet*. Time and space fail one to tell a tithe of the stories of valor and hardship linked in the medals and wounds borne by men on this unostentatious parade — a parade the members of which have shed their blood on the soil of every quarter of the globe. The minutest military annals scarcely name some of the obscure combats in which men here to-day have have fought and bled. This man desperately wounded at Najou, near Shanghai; that one wounded in two places at Owna, in Persia: this one with a sleeve emptied at Aroga, in Abyssinia — who among us remember aught, if, indeed, we have ever heard, of Najou, Owna, or Aroga? On the breast of this bent, hoary old man, note these strange emblems, the Cross of San Fernando and the Order of the Tower and Sword. Their wearer is a relic of the British Legion in the Carlist war of 1837, and they were won under brave old De Lacy Evans at the siege of Bilbao.

Over the modest portals of the Commissionaire Barracks in the Strand might well be inscribed the legend, "To all the military glories of Britain." But just as we have barely a decade ago seen the pride of a palace in another land, on whose façade is a kindred inscription, abased by the occupation of a foreign conqueror, so there was a time when the living emblems of Britain's military glory were wont to undergo much humiliation and adversity when their career of soldiering had come to a close. Germany recompenses her veterans by according them, as a right, reputable civilian employ when they have served their time as soldiers; the custom of Britain, on the contrary, has been to leave her scarred and war-worn soldiers to their own resources, and a pension on which to live is impossible. We were always ready enough to feel a glow of pride at the achievements of our arms; but till lately we were prone to reckon the individual soldier as a social pariah, and to regard the fact of a man's having served in the ranks as a brand of discredit. To this estimate, it must be allowed, the ex-soldier himself very often contributed not a little. Destitute of a future, and often debarred by wounds or by broken health from any laborious industrial employment, he made the most of the present; and his idea of making the most of the future not unfrequently took the form of beer and shiftlessness. Recognizing the disadvantages that bore so hard on the deserving old soldier, recognizing, too, in the words of the late Sir John Burgoyne, that " there are many qualities peculiar to the soldier and sailor, and imbibed by him in the ordinary course of his service, which, added to good character and conduct, may render such men more eligible than others for various services in civil life," Captain Edward Walter founded the Corps of Commissionaires. That organization, beginning with seven men, has now a strength of over five hundred, and its ranks are still open to all the eligible recruits who choose to come forward. The Commissionaire is no recipient of charity: what Captain Walter has done is simply to show him how he may earn an honest and comfortable livelihood, and to provide him, if he desires it, with a home of a kind which the ex-militaire naturally most appreciates. The advantages are open to him of a savings bank and of a sick and burial fund, and when the evil days come when he can no longer earn his own bread, the "Retiring Fund" guarantees the thrifty and steady Commissionaire against the prospect of ending his days in the workhouse. Among the fruits of Captain Walter's devoted and gratuitous services in this cause has been a wholesome change in the bias of popular opinion as to the worth of old soldiers. No longer are they regarded as the mere chaff and *débris* of the cannon fodder — "no account men" as Bret Harte has it; he has furnished them with opportunity to prove, and they have proved, that they can so live and so work as to win the respect and trust of their brethren of the civilian world. The man who has done this thing deserves well, not alone of the British army, but of the British nation. He has brought it about that the time has come when most men think with Sir Roger de Coverley; "You must know," says Sir Roger, "I never make use of anybody to row me that has not lost either a leg or an arm. I would rather bate him a few strokes of his oar than not employ an honest man that has been wounded in the Queen's service. If I was a lord or a bishop . . . I would not put a fellow in my livery that had not a wooden leg."

CHRISTMAS NIGHT IN VERY COMMON LODGINGS.

No references are required at the very common lodgings of which I am about to write; the sole requisite for admission lying in the candidate's possession of current coin of the realm to the modest extent of threepence. The possessor of this sum has never far to look, no matter in what part of London he may be, for such accommodation as a threepenny lodging-house will afford him. These institutions abound in Old Pye Street, Orchard Street, and Great Peter Street, Westminster; they are to be found without deep research in the neighborhood of Tottenham Court Road; Mint Street in the Borough consists of nothing else; and Whitechapel, and indeed the East-end generally, is full of these houses, with their curiously mixed population of casual laborers, thieves, and beggars. Mixed as are the inmates, still most of the houses have certain crude specialities of their own. The Irish dock laborer will go where he can find brother Paddies to talk in a broad brogue of the badness of work, and the "ould blaggards of gangers;" the juvenile pickpocket seeks the society of his fellow-apprentices to the trade, the incidents of which are the "beak" and Holloway Prison, the crowning glory whereof Chatham Hulks; the professional beggar gravitates to that house where he can talk "shop," of good rounds and soft-hearted easily-entreated people, of stern, hard-featured folk who reply to solicitations by threats of the police — where he can swear with appreciated unction at the Mendicity officer, and, with the fullest appreciation of the circle, express fervent wishes for something diametrically hostile to the continued vitality of the officials of the Charity Organization Society.

Who has not noticed how empty are the streets of London on Christmas night? Surely, it seems to us, as my guide and I go eastward, that there are few dwellers in the huge hive so sorely worsted in the fight with the world, as not to have a home of some kind, wherein to abide for this Christmas night. Here and there, a wretched street stroller leans on the railing, gazing wearily on the ruddy glow that penetrates through the drawn curtains — listening with a pitiful wistfulness to the cheerful sounds of domestic merriment. The cabmen tire of bootless waiting on the stands, and rattle off homeward to their own Christmas joys in the mews. The policemen are surly and misanthropical, for the time has not yet come for them to stand off and on in the neighborhood of area gates, and eat semi-cold plum pudding under the benignant smiles of the cook. But, as we presently find, Christmas has little effect in thinning the streets of the Eastend. There is no quietude in throbbing, bustling, noisy, sinful Whitechapel. Rosemary Lane, that fragrantly-named thoroughfare of the many odors — containing to the full as much vice as Ratcliff Highway, as much poverty as Bethnal-green or the Isle of Dogs, as many Irish as Tooley Street or Cow Cross Street, besides an infusion peculiar to itself of the low Jew and the lower German element — Rosemary Lane is seething with humanity. The narrow pavements are crowded with drunken sailors and their women, with big, stubbly-bearded Irishmen and little voluble, slatternly Irishwomen; and in front of each of the many public-houses there lounges a curiously aimless crowd, which, having no money to buy drink, and no seeming expectation of being treated by anybody, could be supposed to hang about the portal of the public-house only just to be near some place where drinking was going on. We push open a dirty swing door and find ourselves in a big bare room, having for furniture a couple of forms, a long table on which a big navvy snores as he slumbers, and a little old woman, clad in a novel costume, the chief material of which appears to be old sacks. This interesting female announces herself as the "deputy" of the lodging-house, and proceeds to do the honors of the establishment with condescension and affability. She ushers us into a large back room, in which there are several forms, and a huge bright charcoal fire. On these forms, and around that fire there sit about two dozen men and boys in various stages of dirt and dilapidation. Most appear to be so solicitous on the score of their linen as to keep it out of sight altogether, and several are barefoot. There is not a clean face in the collection. As one looks at them, some sitting there phlegmatically torpid under the influence of the strong heat, others — the later comers — gazing on the glowing fire hungrily as if it were meat and drink to them as well as heat — as one looks at them, I say, the misty notion comes up, that one had somewhere or other seen every one of them before. Every face seems familiar. But it is only the type of the face that is familiar. Are not all non-society shoeblacks cast in the same mould — lanky, thin-lipped, narrow-shouldered, big-footed, shambling lads, with pear-shaped heads, tallowy faces streaked with blacking, little Tartar eyes, no eyebrows, voices something between the cracked hoarseness of an omnibus driver's and the shrill cry of a child? Might not that odd boy that springs from the gutter somehow to hold a horse, shut a cab-door, or offer to carry a carpet-bag, be the only one of the species, for aught that you are able to distinguish between him and the lad who volunteered the same office half an hour ago three miles away? Is there any individuality in a "got no work to do" cadger to distinguish him from his fellow-howlers, or might it not be supposed that the whole crew had been manufactured in fulfilment of an order from some eccentric experimenter in the *genus homo?* No doubt there do exist diverse minor characteristics whereby Jem the shoeblack can be distinguished by the more intimate of his acquaintance from Mike the shoeblack, but I confess I cannot master the individualities; all I can do is to recognize the type.

No Christmas merriment here — only the great red fire, and the blank dirty faces gazing vacantly upon it. Let us search for joviality in the dingy little court behind, apportioned out into single small rooms, each occupied by a family. A merry Christmas, truly, for this sick Irishman lying in solitude upon the rickety, dilapidated four-poster. He announces himself "most bruck intirely wid rheumatics." Has he a wife? No, she is dead, and has left him "wid four childher." And where are they? There "was two ov thim beyant here in the bed;" the eldest girl had "gone bad," and had left the dingy home for the dingy street;

and he himself was lying here helpless, hungry, penniless, looking at the gradually blackening embers of his last penn'orth of coals. In another room sits a middle-aged Irishwoman, brooding alone in the darkness over a tiny scrap of fire. Her husband is in prison, the "childer" are in the gutter, and she is almost fierce in her abrupt despairing replies to any questioning. Another room shows a very different scene. It is no bigger nor better than any of the rest, — a mere slip of a room, with the rough brickwork of the walls standing out nakedly. There is little in it to boast of in the way of furniture — something which by a stretch of imagination might be taken to be a bedstead, unless it were a couple of hardly-dealt-with clothes-horses; a plank for a table, an upturned pail with the bottom out, and a candle stuck in a bottle. But on the pail without the bottom there sits a cheerful fellow, in a smock, and with a child on each knee, each child sucking an orange as if its life depended on the exhaustion of the juice. On the floor opposite, and with her back to the wall, sits the mother of the family, with a tiny baby on her lap, to which she is chirruping merrily as it sucks. They are keeping Christmas, bless us all; they have a bit of holly over the fireplace, on the table stands a can with the best part of a pint of porter in it, and a plate on which there are three oranges, an apple, and quite a dozen nuts. Who could fail to be jolly with these profuse aids to conviviality? Not the honest fellow in the smock, certainly; frankly owning that work is pretty steady, thank God for it! Not the matron on the floor certainly, as she wipes her mouth on the back of her hand after a pull at the can, although she does give vent to a mysteriously mournful reference to the phenomenon of two Sundays in the same week. Not the children certainly, whose powers of suction as applied to orange juice seem unlimited, and whose faces bear traces of a previous indulgence in the luxury of treacle. "Herbs" is an elastic term; can it be strained to include porter and oranges? If so, here is another proof how truly spoke the Wise Man when he said, "Better is a dinner of herbs where love is, than a stalled ox and hatred therewith."

On our way out into the street again, we are intercepted by an individual who I should have conjectured, had I met him in the vicinity of a potato-field, to be a scarecrow suddenly endowed with vitality. He wears a coat the collar of which reaches nearly to the crown of his head, while its tail hangs all round in a diversified series of ribbons. His trousers, or at least the article of costume to which by courtesy that appellation might be applied, are artistically fastened over one shoulder outside the coat by means of a bit of spun yarn. One leg of these trousers terminates somewhat irregularly in the region of a very dirty knee; the other leg has never began at all, in view of which it is regarded as a special blessing that this interesting member of society has only one leg. The face, not half a bad one — full of rollicking fun and devil-may-care humor; about as impudent an eye as ever I chanced to see; and a mouth, the dimensions of which favor the dire misgiving that the fellow in a sudden access of cannibalistic hunger has eaten his own missing leg, are among this gentleman's facial characteristics. Having introduced himself as "a Jack in the Water for the last twenty years" — an aquatic sphere of life which certainly had produced infinitesimal results on his personal cleanliness — he proceeds with extraordinary volubility to deliver a series of observations, the gist of which, divested of flowers of oratory, is the undeniable assertion that this is Christmas time, and that the present company would have inexpressible gratification in at once commemorating the festive period and our visit by drinking our healths. Jack's oratory is so stimulating as to stir his phlegmatic mates to the pitch of a half hopeful, half despondent exclamation, " Ay, that we should, surely ! " In return for a shilling we receive a blessing from Jack comprehensive enough to include all possible contingencies, and we leave the company trying to settle the knotty question who is trustworthy enough to be sent for the beer with a reasonable prospect of returning.

From Rosemary Lane our next mark is Flower-and-Dean Street, looking into some of the choice spots of Whitechapel on our way. An idea exists in the public mind that any rash individual who should dare to visit Flower-and-Dean Street might indeed come out alive, but would emerge pillaged in a manner so wholesale, that he might be thankful his whiskers and toe-nails were left on. I remember, when on my way to Flower-and-Dean Street on the occasion of my first visit, picturing myself returning to the haunts of civilization stripped, and considerately furnished instead of my clothes with a double supplement of the *Times*, which I had been given to understand was the Flower-and-Dean Street sacrifice on the altar of public decency. But I found out that Flower-and-Dean Street, like a certain gentleman who shall be nameless, is not half so bad as it is called, and there are not a few much worse places in London. Much worse, for instance, is that court out of Whitechapel High Street into which we strike on our way to Flower-and-Dean Street. In the dingy bar of a low public-house, half-a-dozen haggard, gin-sodden, dishevelled women are fighting and cursing, yelling oaths at each other, that make one's blood run cold, as they tear each other's hair and rend the rags off each other's bosoms. The foremost she-demon in the fray carries a child — a tiny baby with lack-lustre eyes and pale pinched face — tucked negligently under one arm, while she deals execution impartially all round with the other. Just across the court, not twenty steps from this devilry, there stands a low-roofed brick edifice, whence comes the sounds of sacred music. Pushing open a swing door we find ourselves in a schoolroom among a devout congregation of the poorest of the poor, gathered here to hold their Christmas prayer meeting. In the earlier part of the day a good dinner, we are told, had been given in the ugly schoolroom to 250 children, regular attendants at this unostentatious but deserving charity. As we step out, a gush of rude but earnest melody flows through the open door into the squalid court to do strange un-Christmas-like combat with the graceless din of the public-house.

A step or two further, and we enter a street of a character so bad, that the two policemen standing at the corner volunteer the business-like caution that we should button up our pockets and mind our eye. Whatever it may be on other nights, this thoroughfare, with so bad a name, is quiet and safe enough on this particular night. Crossing a narrow yard, we open a door and stand face to face with a very curious scene. Two big rooms had been thrown into one by the simple expedient of knocking down the partition. The original fireplaces have been maintained, which, piled high with glowing coke, shed a Rembrandtesque shadow-gleam over the room. There are no other lights. On forms all round the room sit men and women very orderly and quiet, sober enough to all appearance, and with nothing in truth to make them otherwise. The men rough, unkempt, and shaggy as they are, seem fellows who earn their bread by the sweat of their brow. They have not that oblong snake-head and lissom supple lankiness of the professional thief; on the contrary, most are brawny, square-built, and hairy, and a good many have the aspect of countrymen. Of the women, the less said perhaps the better. There is nothing improper in their demeanor, but more imbruted faces I never looked upon. Heavy-jowled and short-necked, beetle-browed and small-eyed, with no one trace of comeliness in any feature, it is a mystery to me who they are and how they live. The answer is ready in that curious circumlocution which seems a set phrase in the East-end — "They go out into the streets to get their living." Presently, as we sit quietly in the background, the coarsest-looking of the women — a female with no forehead to speak of, and with a jaw underhung like that of a bull-dog — begins to sing. What? think you. Of all the songs in the world that one would expect to hear in a threepenny lodging-house in Whitechapel, perhaps the last would be — "When I mingled in the throng of the happy and the gay." The effect at first is supremely ludicrous; but the woman, spite of her stolid face, can sing, and she really puts expression and feeling into her voice. But what a pathos of bitter mockery there wails through the refrain — "'Tis hard to give the hand where the heart can never be!" These poor mercenary trulls, the sport, the scorn, the footballs of the vilest of the vile, singing a sentimental chorus as if they really felt the meaning of the words — as if for them they could have any meaning! Before she began to sing, the vocalist had given a babe she had in her lap to a little beggar-woman with a huge coal-scuttle bonnet. This Mother-Hubbard-looking oddity brings the little child down to one end of the room, so that I notice easily what a beautiful little creature it is, with a halo of golden hair round its head, plump dimpled arms, and a mouth like a rosebud. I ask, staggered in my belief in hereditary physiognomy, whether the woman who had sung is the mother of the child. "Lord, no sir!" replies Mother Bunch, "its mammy's dead these three months, and we're looking arter it among us. It belongs to the house." I must say it does the house much credit, both as regards its personal appearance and its dress.

In another house in the same street we find a considerable number of children living with their parents in these strangely undomestic quarters. A man, who says he is a regular laborer at one of the wharves, has three decently clad, and seemingly well-cared-for children, and his wife is certainly no slattern. He tells me that he pays 3s. 6d. a week for his quarters. I express my surprise that, since that money would procure him a couple of decent rooms in a private house, he does not commence housekeeping on his own account. He has his reasons. First he has not money enough to buy furniture; secondly, his present arrangements save him fire, light, and the cost of cooking apparatus; and thirdly, he likes company. Without being altogether prepared to disagree with him on the broad merits of his last argument, I feel decidedly at issue with him in the particular circumstances of the case. One or two of these I may allude to. A man without a shirt, and except by a polite fiction without a coat as well, is cooking with a toasting fork a strange substance, that seems a cross between a carrot and a kidney. At the other end of the room a brawny fellow, mad drunk, is struggling in the grasp of some half-dozen people, who are restraining him, at the cost of severe disintegration of his clothing, from carrying into effect a series of somewhat vague but desperately sanguine threats fulminated apparently against creation generally. He breaks loose as we stand by and runs a-muck down the room, without, however, materially disturbing the equanimity of the inmates, who seem to regard the episode as rather a matter of course than the contrary.

Hitherto I had seen no great demonstrations in the way of Christmas merry-making; but in the next house we enter, a blind fiddler (a public character who uses his wife instead of a dog to lead him about) is discoursing dance music to his fellow lodgers. The venerable melodist had got drunk all over with the exception of his "bow arm," and that had reached the spasmodic stage, so that the company may be said to be dancing under difficulties. Apart from the fitful and uncertain character of the music, there are other conditions that might discourage any save the most enthusiastic. A gentleman has thought proper to lie down and go to sleep in the very centre of the limited clear space, and the alternatives of nimbly hopping

over him, as if the dance were "Gillie Callum," and
the prostrate man the cross-swords, or of doing the
double-shuffle on any reasonably eligible portion of his
body that might present itself, are neither of them
favorable to a successful worship of Terpsichore.
Again public opinion seems to be in an extremely
rudimentary state on the subject of the figures of the
dance, or, indeed, as to the dance itself. Everybody,
male and female alike, is evidently quite at home in a
jig, and considers it his or her sheet anchor; but when
the jig comes to be complicated by a distant resemblance
to a Scotch reel, still further confused by what appears
to be a vague and partial prompting to do the "Ladies
chain," and finally resolving itself into what by a lively
imagination may be mistaken for a country dance, the
services of an efficient master of the ceremonies are
obviously imperatively required. The dance, as it
seems, is a standing institution, the participants fitfully varying. A girl dances herself out of breath by
an ecstatic saltatory performance based upon the clog
hornpipe, and sinks back gasping on a seat — "*lassata
necdum satiata.*" But, Hydra-like, other girls spring
up and fill the vacuum, so that the floor is always full.
A number of old women, some of them among the
most known "canters" and "mummers" of the
metropolis, sit gazing on the scene with quiet contentment, smiling occasionally at some feat of agility.
This house, it appears, is specially patronized by these
respected and industrious females; a room is set apart
for a dozen of them on the ground floor, so that their
asthma and rheumatism may not be tried by the ascen-
sion of staircases; and the old termagants squabble
and spit at each other like so many cats. The lodg-

ing-house formula is as follows:—"Rather fifty men than twenty women—rather twenty young women than ten old women."

The largest common lodging-house in the East of London is in Thrawl Street, Whitechapel. It is dignified with the name of "Chambers," consists of seven houses thrown into one, and has accommodation for 300 lodgers. The charge is fourpence a night, and the great majority of inmates (all men) are of the honest working class, or at least not professional lawbreakers. The house is a credit to its conductor. The cooking apparatus is of the most serviceable kind, including a number of the most recent improvements. There is a capital reading-room, supplied with a number of newspapers and periodicals, and fitted with comfortably cushioned seats. Church service is conducted every Sunday in the great coffee-room, an apartment more than a hundred feet long. Here are collected the great majority of the inmates, mostly engaged in the absorption of the fifty gallons of porter which is the landlord's Christmas-box. It is here I meet the only Scot I encounter in the night's tour. He is a tall, gray, dilapidated man, with a hook nose, and hair and beard that look as if rats make a practice of gnawing these appendages. He is sitting on a table, laboriously darning his rags, every now and then dropping his needle that he may scratch himself with the more freedom. He is by no means proud, and accepts a cigar with marked urbanity. He had once been a lawyer in a Scotch town, and had neglected the wise precaution of keeping separate his own and his clients' money. Then he had come to London and tried a variety of expedients, having had a finger in a good many pies, from company promoting to publishing prospectuses of unexecuted literary works. Then came bad times and Whitecross Street, and there followed fast, as he says with a grim smile and an extra scratch— "*Faucilis descensus Auvernee.*" But he is buoyant in his rags — if he could only get a decent suit. and find somebody to lend him £10, "on the security of landed property" (which landed property appears to consist of an old instrument of Seisin, dirty enough to plant potatoes on, which he produces from his pocket with the air of a man who had a stake in the country), he has an abiding conviction that all would yet come right, and that ere long he would be rolling in wealth. Finding me indisposed to embark in a transaction based upon the portable "landed security" referred to, he borrows half-a-crown. for which he scrupulously gives his I O U, making the same out in duplicate, and bestowing one copy on me, while he carefully inserts the other within the "landed security." and resumes contentedly his darning and scratching.

Not to speak of the Scotsman, there is no lack of character here. A big man, with a broken nose, had attached himself to me when I first entered, and is most assiduous in doing the honors of the place. In a sequestered passage he becomes confidential, and with a mysterious nod says, in a hoarse whisper, "I'm the famous Billy Waters."

As it is obvious that not to know who is the "famous Billy Waters" is tantamount to a confession of dense ignorance, I mutter something expressive of my profound delight at being permitted to contemplate with the naked eye an individual so distinguished. The great man must see through my assumption of knowledge, for with a wink in which the modesty of the hero and the natural pride of the man struggle for the mastery, he continues,

"I'm the teetotal pugilist."

I may be pardoned for the acknowledgment that this announcement strikes me dumb. Seeing his advantage, Mr. Waters, in a tone of suppressed triumph, asks —

"Would you like to see me drink a bucket o' water? I'll do it for a bob. I drank two once at Newmarket, but that was long ago, to please the Markis, an' he'd chucked a sov. into the bottom of each bucket."

When such a fact is taken into consideration, Mr. Waters' present offer may be considered dirt cheap; but I venture to decline it, whereupon he withdraws himself in unconcealed disgust at a man so lost to a sense of the fitness of things as to decline paying a "bob" to see another man drink a bucket of water.

In Flower-and-Dean Street, at length reached after many deviations and delays, every house is a common lodging-house, and there is licensed accommodation in it for no fewer than 1,500 occupants. The first house we entered seems tenanted chiefly by boys and lads, and by women. Many of the former are mere children, dirt begrimed youngsters of the bootblack, fusee-selling, and thieving classes. The women, almost without exception, are in the lowest condition of degradation. One is lying on the floor in a drunken sleep, with her head so close to the fire that it is difficult to resist the impression that she is being roasted. The boys are squatting on the floor all around her, drinking and smoking — even the youngest of them — as if they were bearded men. I ask one of the biggest to pull the woman back. "Oh, she be ——," is the reply; "let her cook, and we'll eat her for supper." As he speaks, the woman scrambles to her feet — a mass of rags, blowzy flesh, and dishevelled hair — and staggering to the door, rolls herself down in the gutter, where, as we pass out, she seems fast asleep again.

Most of the houses in Flower-and-Dean Street are profusely decorated with festoons of colored paper, hanging across the windows, and from point to point along the low-pitched roof. In these houses mostly live the women whom we see about the streets selling fire ornaments, Chinese lanterns, and cut papers of divers colors, and it appears that they have devoted their spare time to the adornment of their "respective places of abode." In the last house we enter the decorations are of an especially gorgeous kind. Several dozens of illuminated Chinese lamps hang from the ceiling, and all the other lights are extinguished. This establishment boasts of a regular chairman in the person of a glib-tongued young thief, who, seated in state upon the table, in good set phrase fines me 6d. for daring to come into his presence with my hat on. As we turn out into the dirty stinking street the sounds of revelry seem to wax louder and louder as we recede from them. an acoustic phenomenon for which a policeman sagely accounts in the observation, "They're warming to it now; by twelve o'clock a good half on 'em will be blazing drunk."

HOW I "SAVED FRANCE."

THESE be big words, my masters! I can only say they are not mine — I am far too modest to utter any such high-sounding phrase on my own responsibility — but they are the exact terms used by a high municipal dignitary in characterizing the result of what he was pleased to term my " chivalrous conduct." My sardonic chum, on the contrary, — an individual wholly abandoned to the ignoble vice of punning — asserts that my conduct was simply "barbarous." It will be for the reader to judge.

St. Meuse — let us call it St. Meuse — is a town of what is still French Lorraine; and to St. Meuse I came drifting up the Marne Valley, over the flat expanse of the plain of Chalons, and by St. Menehould, the proud stronghold of pickled pig's feet, in the second week of September, 1873. St. Meuse was one of the last of the French cities held in pawn by the Germans for the payment of the milliards. The last instalment of the blood-money had been paid, and the *Pickelhaubes* were about to evacuate St. Meuse, as soon as the cash had been methodically counted, and after they should have leisurely filled their baggage trains and packed their portmanteaus. My intention in going to St. Meuse was to witness this evacuation scene, and to be a spectator of the return of light-heartedness to the French population, on the withdrawal of the Teuton incubus which for three years had lain upon the safety valve of their constitutional sprightliness. I had been a little out in my reckoning of time, and, when I reached St. Meuse, I found that I had a week to stay there before the event should occur which I had come to witness; but the interval could not be regarded as lost time, for St. Meuse is a very pleasant city, and the conditions which were so soon to terminate, presented a most interesting field of study.

You must know that St. Meuse is a fortress. It has a citadel, or at least such fragments of a citadel as a bombardment has left, and the quaint old town is surrounded with bastions which are linked by curtains, and flanked by lunettes, the whole being girdled by a ditch, beyond the counterscarp of which speads a sloping glacis, which makes a very pleasant promenade. The defensive strength of the place is reduced to zero in these days of far-reaching rifled siege artillery, for it lies in a cup, and is surrounded on all sides by hills, the summits of which easily command the fortifications. But the consciousness that it is obsolete as a fortress has not yet come home to St. Meuse. It has, in truth, a very good opinion of itself as a valorous, not to say heroic, place: nor can it be denied that its title to this self-complacency has been fairly earned. In the Franco-German war, spite of its defects, it stood a siege of over two months, and succumbed only after a severe bombardment which lasted for several days. And while as yet it was not wholly beleaguered, it was very active in making itself disagreeable to the foreign invader. It was a patrolling party from St. Meuse that intercepted the courier on his way from the battle-field of Sedan to Germany, carrying the hurried lines to his wife which the Crown Prince of Prussia scrawled on the fly-leaf of an orderly book while as yet the last shots of the combat were dropping in the distance; carrying too the notes of the momentous battle which William Howard Russell had jotted down in the heat of the action, and took the first opportunity of despatching. St. Meuse, then, had balked the Princess of the first tidings of her husband's safety, and the great English newspaper of the earliest details of the most sensational battle of the age. It had fallen at last, but not ingloriously, and the iron of defeat had not entered so deeply into its soul as had been the case with some French fortresses, of which it could not well be said that they had done their honest best to resist their fate. Its self-respect, at least, was left to it, and it was something to know that when the German garrison should march away it was bound to leave to St. Meuse the artillery and munitions of war of the fortress, just as they had been found on the day of the surrender.

I came to like St. Meuse immensely in the course of the days I spent in it waiting for the great event of the evacuation. The company at the table d'hôte of the Trois Maures was varied and amusing. The Germans ate in a room by themselves, so that the obnoxious element was not present overtly at the general table d'hôte. But we had a few German officials in plain clothes — clerks in General Manteuffel's bureau, contractors, cigar merchants, &c. — who spoke French even among themselves, and were painfully polite to the French habitués, who were as painfully polite in return. There was a batch of Parisian journalists who had come to St. Meuse to watch the evacuation, and who wrote their letters in the café over the way to the accompaniment of *verres* of *absinthe*, and bocks of beer. Then there was the gallant Captain of Gensdarmes, who had arrived with a trusty band of twenty-five subordinates, to take over from the Germans the municipal superintendence of the place, and, later, the occupation of the fortress. He was the most polite man I ever knew, this Captain of Gensdarmes, with a clever knack of turning you outside in in the course of half an hour's conversation, and the peculiar attribute of having to all appearance eyes in the back of his head. To him, as he placidly ate his food, there came, from time to time, quiet and rather bashful-looking men in civilian attire of a slightly seedy description. Sometimes they merely caught his eye and went out again without speaking; sometimes they handed to him little notes; sometimes they held with him a brief whispered conversation, during which the captain's nonchalance was imperturbable. These respectable individuals who, if they saw you once in conversation with their chief, ever after bowed to you with the greatest *empressement*, were members of the secret police.

As for the inhabitants of St. Meuse, they appeared to await the hour of their delivery with considerable philosophy. Physically they are the finest race I ever saw in France, their men tall, square, and muscular, their women handsome and comely. Numbers of both sexes are fair-haired, and the sandiness of hair which we are wont to associate with the Scottish Celt is by no means uncommon. A sardonic companion, whom I had picked up by the way, attributed those characteristics to the fact that in the great war, St. Meuse was a depôt for British prisoners of war, who had in some way contrived to imbue the native population with some of their own physical attributes. He further prophesied a wave of Teuton characteristics as the result of the German occupation which was about to terminate; but his insinuations seemed to me to partake of the scurrilous, especially as he instanced Lewes, a British depôt for foreign prisoners of war, as a field in which similar phenomena were to be discerned. But, nevertheless, I unquestionably found a good deal of what may be called national hybridism in St. Meuse. I used to buy photographs of a shopkeeper over whose door was blazoned the Scottish name Macfarlane. Outwardly Macfarlane was a "hielanman" all over. He had a shock-head of bright red hair such as might have thatched the poll of the "Dougal cratur;" his cheek-bones were high, his nose of the Captain of Knockdunder pattern, and his mouth of true Celtic amplitude. One felt intuitively as if Macfarlane were bound to know Gaelic, and that the times were out of joint when he evinced greater fondness for *eau sucrée* than for Talisker. It was with quite a sense of dislocation of the fitness of things that I found Macfarlane could talk nothing but French. But although he had torn up the ancient landmarks, or rather suffered them to lapse, he yet was proud of his ancestry. His grandfather, it appeared, was a soldier of the "Black Watch," who had been a prisoner of war in St. Meuse, and who when the peace came had preferred taking unto himself a daughter of the Amalekite, and settling in St. Meuse, to going home to a pension of sevenpence a day and liberty to ply as an Edinburgh cadie.

As for the German "men in possession," they pursued the even tenor of their way in the precise, yet phlegmatic German manner. Their guards kept the gates and bridges as if they meant to hold the place till the crack of doom, instead of being under orders to clear out within the week. The recruits drilled on the citadel esplanade — straightening their legs and pointing their toes, as if their sole ambition in life was to kick their feet away into space, down to the very eve of evacuation. Their battalions practised skirmishing on the glacis with that routine assiduity which is the secret of the German military success. Old Manteuffel was living in the prefecture, holding his levees and giving his stiff ceremonious dinner parties, as if he had done despite to Dr. Cumming's warnings and taken a lease of the place. The German officers thronged their café, each man, after the manner of German officers, shouting at the pitch of his voice; and at the café of the under-officers tough old wachtmeisters and grizzled sergeants with many medals played long quiet games at cards or knocked the balls about on the chubby little pocketless tables with cues, the tips of which were as large as the base of a six-pounder shell.

The French journalists insisted I should accept it as an article of faith that these two races dwelling together in St. Meuse hated each other like poison. They would have it that while discipline alone prevented the Germans from massacring every Frenchman in the place, it was only a humiliating sense of weakness that hindered the Frenchmen from rising in hot fury against the Germans who were their temporary masters. I am afraid the gentlemen of the Parisian press came rather to dislike me on account of my obdurate scepticism in such matters. That there was no great cordiality was obvious and natural. Some of the Germans were arrogant and domineering. For instance, having a respect for the Germans, it pained and indeed disgusted me, to hear a colonel of the German staff, in answer to my question whether the evacuating force would march out with a rear guard as in war-time, reply, "Pho, a Field-Gendarme with a whip is rear-guard enough against such *canaille!*" But in the mouths of Hans and Carl and Johann, the stout *Kerle* of the ranks, there were no such words of bitter scorn for their compulsory hosts. The honest fellows drew water for the goodwives on whom they were billeted, did a good deal of stolid love-making with the girls, and nursed the babies with a solicitude that put to shame the male parents of these youthful hopes of Troy. I take leave, as a reasonable man, to doubt whether it can lie in the heart of a family to hate a man who has dandled its baby, and whether a man can be rancorous against a family whose baby he has nursed. But fashion's sway is omnipotent in emotion as in dress. Ever since the war, journalists, authors, and public opinion generally had hammered it into the French nation, that if it were not to be a traitor to its patriotism, the first article of its creed must be hatred against the German, and that the bitterer this hate, the more fervent the patriotism. It was not indeed incumbent on French men and French women to accept this creed, but it behooved them at least to profess it; and it must be admitted that they did this for the most part with an intensity and vigor which seemed to prove that with many profession had deepened into conviction.

While as yet the evacuation had been a thing of the

remote future, the people of St. Meuse had borne the yoke lightly, and indeed had, I believe, privily congratulated themselves on the substantial advantages, in the way of money spent in the place and the immunity from taxation, which were incidental to the foreign occupation. But as the day for the evacuation drew closer and closer, one became dimly conscious of an electrical condition of the social atmosphere, which any trifle might stimulate into a thunder-storm. Blouses gathered and muttered about the street corners, scowling at and elbowing the German soldiers as they strode to buy sausages to stay them in the homeward march. The gamins, always covertly insolent, no longer cloaked their insolence and wagged little tricolor flags under the nose of the stolid German sentry on the Pont St. Croix. At the table d'hôte the painful politeness of the German civilians had no effect in thawing the studied coldness of the French habitués.

As for myself, I was a neutral, and professing to take no side, flattered myself that I could keep out of the vortex of the soreness. Soon after my arrival at St. Meuse I had called upon his worship the Mayor at his official quarters in the Hôtel de Ville, and had received civil speeches in return for civil speeches. Then I had left my card on General Manteuffel, with whom I happened to have a previous acquaintance, and those formal duties of a benevolent neutral having been performed, I had held myself free to choose my own company. Circumstances had some time before brought me into familiar contact with very many German officers, and I had imbibed a liking for their ways and conversation, noisy as the latter is. Several of the officers then in St. Meuse had been personal acquaintances in other days, and it was at once natural and pleasant for me to renew the intercourse. I was made an honorary member of the mess: I spent many hours in the officers' casino, I rode out with the officers of the squadron of Uhlans. All this was very pleasant; but as the day of the evacuation became close, I noticed that the civility of the French Captain of Gensdarmes grew colder, that the cordiality of the French·habitués of the table d'hôte visibly diminished, and that I encountered not a few unfriendly looks when I walked through the streets by myself. It began to dawn upon me that St. Meuse was getting to reckon me a German sympathizer, and, as there was no halfway house, therefore not in accord with the emotions of France and St. Meuse.

On the afternoon immediately preceding the morning that had been fixed for the evacuation, there came to me a polite request that I should visit M. le Maire at the Hôtel de Ville. His worship was elaborately civil but obviously troubled in mind. He coughed nervously several times, after the initiatory compliments had passed, and then began to speak.

"Monsieur, you are aware that the Germans are going to-morrow morning?"

I replied that I had cognizance of this fact.

"Do you also know that the last of the German civilian officials depart by the five A.M. train, not caring to remain here after the troops are gone?"

Of this also I was aware.

"Let me hope," continued the Mayor, "that you are going along with them, or, at all events, will ride away with Messieurs the soldiers?"

On the contrary, was my reply, I had come not

alone to witness the evacuation, but to note how St. Meuse should bear herself in the hour of her liberation: I desired to witness the rejoicings: I was not less anxious to be a spectator of any disturbance, if such unhappily should occur. Why should M. le Maire have conceived this desire to balk my natural curiosity?

M. le Maire was obviously not a little embarrassed; but he persevered and was candid. This deplorable occupation was now so nearly finished, and happily, as yet, every thing had been so tranquil, that it would be a thousand pities if any untoward event should occur to detract from the dignified attitude which the evacuated territory had maintained. It was of critical importance in every sense that St. Meuse should not give way to riot or disorder on that occasion. He hoped and believed it would not — here M. le Maire laid his hand on his heart — but a spark, as I knew, fired tinder, and the St. Meuse populace were at present figurative tinder. I might be that spark —

"You much resemble a German," said M. le Maire, "with that great yellow beard of yours, and your broad shoulders, as if you had carried arms. Our citizens have seen you much in the society of Messieurs the German officers; they are not in a temper to draw fine distinctions of nationality; and, dear sir, I ask you to go away with the Germans, lest, perchance, our blouses, reckoning you for a German, should not be very tender with you, when the spiked helmets are out of the place. The truth is," said the worthy Maire, with a burst of plain speaking, "I'm afraid that you will be mobbed, and that there will be a row, and then the Germans may come back, and the evacuation be postponed, and I'll get wigged by the Prefect and the Minister of the Interior, and bully-ragged in the newspapers, and St. Meuse will get abused, and the fat will be generally in the fire!"

Here was an awkward fix. I could not comply with the Mayor's request; that was not to be thought of, for reasons I need not mention here. I had no particular desire to be mobbed. Once before I had experienced the tender mercies of a French mob, and knew that they were very cruel. But stronger than the personal feeling was my sincere sympathy with the Mayor's critical position, and my anxiety, by what means might be within my power, to contribute to the maintenance of a tranquillity so desirable. But then what means were within my power? I could not go; I could not promise to stop indoors, for it was incumbent on me to see every thing that was to be seen. And, if through me trouble came, I should be responsible heaven knows for what! — with a skinful of sore bones into the bargain.

"If Monsieur cannot go" — the Mayor broke in upon my cogitation — "if Monsieur cannot go, will he pardon the exigency of the occasion if I suggest one other alternative? It is" — here the Mayor hesitated — "it is the yellow beard which gives to Monsieur the aspect of a German. With only whiskers nobody could take Monsieur for any thing but an Englishman. If Monsieur would only have the complaisance and charity to — to" —

Cut off my beard! Great powers! shear that mane that had been growing for years! — that cataract of hair that had been, so to speak, my oriflamme; the only physical belonging of which I ever was proud, the only thing, so far as I know, that I had ever been envied! For the moment the suggestion knocked me all of a heap. There came into my head some confused reminiscence of a story about a girl who cut off her hair and sold it to keep her mother from starving, or redeem her lover from captivity, or something of the kind. But that must have been before the epoch of parish relief, and kidnapping is now punishable by statute. What was St. Meuse to me that for her I should mow my hirsute glories? But then, if people got savage, they might pull my beard out by the roots. And there had been lately dawning on me the dire truth that its tawny hue was becoming somewhat freely streaked with gray, a color I abhor, except in eyes. I made up my mind.

"I'll do it, sir," said I to the Mayor, with a manly curtness. My heart was too full for many words.

He respected my emotion, bowed in silence over the hand which he had grasped, and only spoke to give me the address of his own barber.

This barber was a patriot of unquestioned zeal, but I am inclined to think his extraction was similar to that of Macfarlane, for he combined patriotism with profit in a most edifying manner. He shaved the German officers during the whole of their stay in St. Meuse, he accompanied them on their march to the frontier: he earned the last centime in Conflans, and then driving forward to the frontier line, he unfurled the tricolor as the last German soldier stepped over it. It is seldom that one in this world sees his way to being so adroitly ambidextrous.

But this is a digression. In twenty minutes, shorn and shaven, I was back again in the Mayor's parlor.

The tears of gratitude stood in his eyes. I learned afterwards that a decoration was contingent on his preservation of the public peace on the occasion of the evacuation.

Started by the Mayor, the report rapidly circulated through St. Meuse that I had cut off my beard rather than that it should be possible that any one should mistake me for a German. From being a suspect, I became a popular idol. The French journalists entertained me to a banquet at night, at which in libations of champagne, eternal amity between France and England was pledged. Next morning the Germans went away, and then St. Meuse kicked up its heels and burst into exuberant joy. The Mayor took me up to the station in his own carriage to meet the French troops, and introduced me to the colonel of the battalion as a man who had made sacrifices for *la belle France*. The colonel shook me cordially by the hand, and I was embraced by the robust vivandière, who struck me as being in the practice of sustaining life on a diet of garlic. When we emerged from the station I was cheered almost as loudly as was the colonel, and a man waved a tricolor over my head all the way back to the town, treading at frequent intervals on my heels. In the course of the afternoon I happened to approach the civic band, which was performing patriotic music in the Place St. Croix. When the bandmaster saw me he broke off the programme, and struck up "Rule Britannia!" in my honor, to the clamorous joy of the audience, who were thwarted in their aim of carrying me round the Place shoulder-high, only by the constancy with which I clung to the railings which surround Chevert's statue.

But the crowning recognition of my sacrifice came at the banquet which the town gave to the French officers. The Mayor proposed the toast of "Our English Friend." "We had all," he said, "made sacrifices for *la Patrie*, he himself had sustained the loss of a wooden outhouse burned down in the bombardment; the gallant colonel on his right had spilt his blood at St. Privat. Them it behooved to suffer, and they would do it again, for it was as he had said for *la Patrie*. But what was to be said of an honorable gentleman who had sacrificed the most distinguishing ornament of his physical aspect, without the holy stimulus of patriotism, and simply that there might be obviated the risk of an embroilment, to the possible consequences of which he would not further allude? Would it be called the language of extravagant hyperbole, or would they not rather be words justified by the facts, when he ventured before this honorable company to assert that his respected English friend had by his self-sacrifice saved France from a great peril?" The Mayor's question was replied to by a perfect whirlwind of cheering. Everybody in the room insisted upon shaking hands with me, and I was forced to get on my legs and make a reply. Later in the evening I heard the Mayor and the town clerk discussing the project of conferring upon me the freedom of the city.

THE INVERNESS CHARACTER FAIR, 1873.

"THURSDAY. — Gathering, hand-shaking, brandy and soda and drams.

"*Friday.* — Drinking, daundering and feeling the way in the forenoon; the ordinary in the afternoon; at night a spate of drink and bargaining.

"*Saturday.* — Bargaining and drink.

"*Sunday morning.* — Bargains, drink, and the kirk."

Such was the skeleton programme of the Inverness Character Fair given by a farmer friend to me, who happened to be lazily rusticating in the north of Scotland during the pleasant month of July. My friend asked me to accompany him in his visit to this remarkable institution, and the programme was too tempting for refusal. As we drove to the station he handed me Henry Dixon's "Field and Fern," open at a page which gave some particulars of the origin and character of the great annual sheep and wool market of the north. "Its Character Market," writes "The Druid" — no longer, alas! among us — "is the great bucolic glory of Inverness. The Fort William market existed before; but the Sutherland and Caithness men, who sold about 14,000 sheep and 15,000 stones of wool annually so far back as 1816, did not care to go there. They dealt with regular customers year after year, and roving woolstaplers with no regular connection went about and notified their arrival on the church door. Patrick Sellar, 'the agent for the Sutherland Association.' saw exactly that some great *caucus* of buyers and sellers was wanted at a more central spot. and on February 27th. 1817. that meeting of the clans was held at Inverness which brought the fair into being. Huddersfield, Wakefield. Halifax, Burnley. Aberdeen. and Elgin signified that their leading merchants were favorable and ready to attend. Sutherland. Caithness, Wester Ross. Skye. the Orkneys. Harris. and Lewis, were represented at the meeting: Bailie Anderson also 'would state with confidence that the market was approved of by William Chisholm, Esq., of Chisholm, and James Laidlaw, tacksman, of Knockfin;' and so the matter was settled for ever and aye. and the *Courier* and the *Morning Chronicle* were the London advertising media. This Highland wool Parliament was originally held on the third Thursday in June. but now it begins on the second Thursday of July. and lasts till the Saturday; and Argyleshire. Nairnshire. and High Aberdeenshire have gradually joined in. The plainstones in front of the Caledonian Hotel have always been the scene of the bargains, which are most truly based on the broad stone of honor; not a sheep or fleece is to be seen, and the buyer of the year before gets the first offer of the cast or clip. The previous proving and public character of the different flocks are the purchasers' guide far more than the sellers' description."

Thus far "The Druid;" and my companion, as we drove, supplemented his information. It is from the circumstance that not a head of sheep or a tait of wool is brought to the market, but that every thing is sold and bought unseen, and even unsampled, that the market derives its appellation of "character" fair. Of the value of the business transacted — the amount of money turned over — it is impossible to form with any confidence even an approximate estimate, since there is no source for data; but none with whom I spoke put the turn-over at a lower figure than half a million. In a good season, such as the past, over 200,000 sheep are disposed of, exclusive of lambs, and of lambs about the same number. The stock sold from the hills are for the most part Cheviots and blackfaces; from the low grounds half-breds, being a cross between Leicester and Cheviot, and crosses between the Cheviot and blackface. All the sales of sheep and lambs are by the "clad score," which contains twenty-one. The odd one is thrown in to meet the contingency of deaths before delivery is effected. Established when there was a long and wearing journey for the flocks from the hills where they were reared down to their purchasers in the lowlands or the south country, the altered conditions of transit have stimulated farmers to efforts for the abolition of the "clad score." Now that sheep are trucked by railway instead of being driven on foot, or conveyed from the islands to their destination in steamers specially chartered for the purpose, the farmers grudge the "one in" of the "clad score." In 1866 they seized the opportunity of an exceptionally high market and keen competition to combine against the old reckoning, and in a measure succeeded. But next year was as dull as '66 had been brisk, and then the buyers and dealers had their revenge, and re-established the "clad score" in all its pristine firmness of position. The sheep farmers wean their lambs about the 24th of August, and delivery of them is given to the buyers as soon as possible thereafter. The delivery of ewes and wethers is timed by individual arrangement. A large proportion of the old ewes — no ewes are sold but such as are old — go to England, where a lamb or two is got from them before they are fattened. Most of the lambs are bought by sheep farmers, who, not keeping a ewe flock, are not themselves breeders, and are kept till they are three years old — "three shears," as they are technically called — and sold fat into the south country. There they get what Mr. McCombie called the last dip, and the butcher sells them as "prime four-year-old wedder mutton."

The size of some of the Highland sheep farms is to be reckoned by miles, not by acres, and the stock, as in Australia, by the thousand. The largest sheep-owner, perhaps, that the Highlands ever knew was Cameron of Corriehollie, now dead. He was once examined before a Committee of the House of Commons, and came to be questioned on the subject of his ownership of sheep. "You may have some 1,500 sheep, probably, sir?" quoth the interrogating M.P. "Aiblins," was Corriehollie's quiet reply, as he took a pinch of snuff; "Aiblins I have a few more nor that." "Two thousand, then?" "Yes, I pelieve I have that and a few more forpye," calmly responded the Highlander with another pinch. "Five thousand?" "Oh ay, and a few more." "Twenty thousand, sir?" cried the M.P., capping with a burst his previous bid. "Oh ay, and some more forpye," was the imperturbable response of Corriehollie. "In heaven's name, how many sheep have you, man?" burst out the astonished catechist. "I'm no very sure to a thousan' or two," replied Corriehollie, in his dry laconic way, and with an extra big pinch; "but I'm owner of forty thousan' sheep at the lowest reckoning." Lochiel, known to the Sassenach as Mr. Cameron, M.P., is perhaps the largest living sheep-owner in Scotland. He has at least 30,000 sheep on his vast tracks of moorland on the braes of Lochaber. In the island of Skye, Captain Cameron of Talisker has a flock of some 12,000; and there are several other flocks, both in the islands and on the mainland, of more than equal magnitude. Sheep-farming is, at least in many instances, an hereditary avocation, and some families can trace a sheep-farming ancestry very far back. The oldest sheep-farming family in Scotland are the Mackinnons of Corrie, in Skye. They have been on Corrie for four hundred years, and they were holding sheep-farms elsewhere even earlier. The Macraes of Achnagart, in Kintail, have paid rent to Seaforth for two hundred years. For as long before they had held Achnagart on the tenure of a bunch of heather exigible annually and their fighting services as good clansmen. Two hundred years ago an annual rental of £5 was substituted for the heather "corve;" the clansmen's service continuing and being rendered up till the '45. Now clanship is but a name, a Seaforth Mackenzie is no longer chief in Kintail, and the Macrae who has succeeded his forbears in Achnagart finds the bunch of heather and the £5 alike superseded by the very far other than nominal annual rent of a thousand pounds. The modern Achnagart, with his broad shoulders and burly frame, looks as capable as were any of his ancestry to render personal service to his chief if a demand were made upon him; and very probably would be quite prepared to accept a reduction of his money rental if an obligation to perform feudal clan-service were substituted. Achnagart, with his £1,000 a year rental, by no means tops the sheep-farming rentals of his county. Perhaps Robertson of Achiltie, whose sheep-walks stretch up on to the snow-patched shoulders of Ben Wyvis, and far away west to Loch Broom, pays the highest sheep-farming rental in Ross-shire, when the factor has pocketed his half-yearly check for £800.

Part of this I learn from my friend as we drive to the station; part I gather afterwards from other sources. The station for which we are bound is Elgin, the county town of Morayshire. Between Elgin and Inverness, it is true, we shall see but few of the great sheep-farmers and flock-masters of the west country, who converge on the annual tryst from other points of the compass and by various routes — by the Skye Railway, by that portion of the Highland line which extends north of Inverness through Ross into Sutherland, by the Caledonian Canal, &c. But it is promised to me that I shall see many of the notable agriculturists of Moray land, who go to the market as buyers; and a contingent of sheep-breeders are sure to join us at Forres, coming down the Highland line from the Inverness-shire Highlands on Upper Strathspey. There is quite an exceptional throng on the platform of the Elgin Station, of farmers, factors, lawyers and ex-coffee planters — both very plentiful in Elgin; tanners bound for investments in prospective pelts, and men of no avocation, yet as much bound to visit

Inverness to-day as if they meant to invest thousands. In a corner towers the mighty form of Paterson of Mulben, famous among breeders of polls with his tribe of *Mayflowers*. From beneath a kilt peep out the brawny limbs of Willie Brown of Linkwood and Morriston, nephew of stout old Sir George who commanded the light division at the Alma, son to a factor whose word in his day was as the laws of the Medes and Persians over a wide territory, and himself the feeder of the leviathan cross red ox and the beautiful gray heifer which took honors so high at one of the recent Smithfield Christmas Shows. There is the white beard and hearty face of Mr. Collie, late of Ardgay, owner erstwhile of Fair Maid of Perth and breeder of Zarah. Here, too, is a fresh, sprightly gentleman in a kilt, whom his companions designate "the Bourach." Requesting an explanation of the term, I am told that "Bourach" is the Gaelic for "through-other," which again is the Scottish synonyme for a kind of amalgam of addled and harum-scarum. A jolly tanner observes, "I'll get a box to oursels." The reason of the desire for this exclusive accommodation is apparent as soon as we start. A "deck" of cards is produced, and a quartette betake themselves to whist with half-crown stakes on the rubber and sixpenny points. This was mild speculation to that which was engaged in on the homeward journey after the market, when a Strathspey sheep farmer won £8 between Dalvey and Forres. As my friends shuffle and deal, I look out of window at the warm gray towers of the cathedral, beautiful still spite of the desecrating hand of the "Wolf of Badenoch." Our road lies through the fertile "Laigh of Moray," one of the richest wheat districts in the Empire, and as beautiful as fertile. At Alves we pick up a fresh, hale gentleman, who is described to me as "the laird of three properties," bought for more than £100,000 by a man who began life as the son of a hillside crofter. We pass the picturesque ruins of Kinloss Abbey and draw up at Forres Station, whose platform is thronged with noted agriculturists bound for the "Character Fair." Here is that spirited Englishman, Mr. Harris of Earnhill, whose great cross ox took the cup at the Agricultural Hall seven or eight years ago: and the brothers Bruce — he of Newton of Struthers, whose marvellous polled cow beat every thing in Bingley Hall at the '71 Christmas Show, and but for "foot and mouth" would have repeated the performance at the Smithfield Show; and he of Burnside, who likewise has stamped his mark pretty deeply in the latter arena. At Forres we first hear Gaelic; for a train from Carr Bridge and Grantown in Upper Strathspey has come down the Highland Railway to join ours, and the red-haired Grants around the Rock of Craigellachie — where a man whose name is not Grant is regarded as a *lusus naturæ* — are Gaelic speakers to a man. No witches accost us, and speaking personally, I feel no "pricking of the thumbs," as we skirt the blasted heath on which Macbeth met the witches; the most graphic modern description of which on record was given to Henry Dixon in the following quaint form of Shakespearean annotation: "It's just a sort of eminence; all firs and ploughed land now; you paid a toll near it. I'm thinking — it's just a mile wast from Brodie Station."

Nairn is that town by the citation of a peculiarity of

which King Jamie put to shame the boastings of the Southrons as to the superior magnitude of English towns. "I have a town," quoth the sapient James, "in my auncient kingdom of Scotland, whilk is sae lang that at ane end of it a different language is spoken from that whilk prevails at the other." To this day the monarch's words are true; one end of Nairn is Gaelic, the other Sassenach. Here we obtain a numerous accession of strength. The attributes of one kilted chieftain are described to me in curious scraps of illustrative patchwork, "A great litigant, an enthusiastic agriculturist, a dealer in Hielan' nowt — something of a Hielan' nowt himself, a semi-auctioneer, a great hand as chairman at an agricultural dinner, a visitor to the Baker Street Bazaar when the Smithfield Shows were held there, and where the Cockneys mistook him for one of the exhibits, and began pinching and punching him." Stewart of Duntalloch swings his stalwart form into our carriage — a noted breeder of Highland cattle, and as fine a specimen of a Highlander as can be seen from Reay to Pitlochrie. "Culloden!" "Culloden!" chant the porters in that curious sing-song peculiar to the Scotch platform porter. The whistle of the engine and the talk about turnips and cattle contrast harshly with that bleak, lonely moorland swell yonder — the patches of green among the brown heather telling where moulders the dust of the chivalrous clansmen. It is not a great while longer than a century ago, since Charles Stuart and Cumberland confronted each other over against us there; and here are the descendants of the men that fought in their tartans for the "King over the Water," who are discussing the right proportion of phosphates in artificial manures, and of whom one asks me confidentially for my opinion on the Leger favorite.

Here we are at Inverness at length: that city of the Clachnacudden stone. There is quite a crowd in the spacious station of business people who have been awaiting the arrival of the train from the east, and the buyers and sellers whom it has conveyed find themselves at once among eager friends. Hurried announcements are made as to the condition and prospects of the market. The card-players have plunged suddenly *in medias res* of bargaining. The man who had volunteered to stand me a seltzer and sherry has forgotten all about his offer, and is talking energetically about clad scores and the price of lambs. I quit the station, and walk up Union Street, through a gradually thickening throng, till I reach Church Street, and shoulder my way to the front of the Caledonian Hotel. I am now in "the heart of the market," standing as I am on the plainstones in front of the Caledonian Hotel, and looking up and down along the crowded street. What physique, what broad shoulders, stalwart limbs, wiry red beards and high cheek-bones there are everywhere! You have the kilt at every turn, in every tartan, and often in no tartan at all. Other men wear whole-colored suits of inconceivably shaggy tweed, and the breadth of the bonnets is only equalled by that of the accents. Every second man has a mighty plaid over his shoulder. It may serve as a sample of his wool, for invariably it is home made. Some carry long twisted crooks, such as we see in old pastoral prints; others have massive gnarled sticks grasped in vast sinewy hands, on the back of which the wiry red hairs stand out like prickles. There is falling what in the south we should reckon as a very respectable pelt of rain, but the Inverness Wool Fair heeds rain no more than thistledown. Hardly a man has thought it worth his pains to envelop his shoulders in his plaid, but stands and lets the rain take its chance. There is a perfect babel of tongues: no bawling or shouting, however, but a perpetual gruff *susurrus* of broad guttural conversation, accentuated every now and then by a louder exclamation in Gaelic. Quite half of the throng are discoursing in this language. It is possible to note the difference in the character of Celt and Teuton. The former gesticulates, splutters out a perfect torrent of alternately shrill, guttural, and intoned Gaelic; he shrugs his shoulders, he throws his arms about, he thrills with vivacity. The Teuton expresses quiet, sententious canniness in every gesture and every utterance; he is a cool-blooded man, and keeps his breath to cool his porridge.

On the plainstones there are a number of benches, on which men sit down to gossip and chaffer. Scraps of dialogue float about in the moist air. If you care to be an eaves-dropper you must have a knowledge of Gaelic to be one effectively. "It's to be a stout market," remarks stalwart Macrae of Invershiel, come of a fine old West Highland stock, and himself a very large sheep-farmer. "Sixteen shillings is my price. I'll come down a little if you like," says young Asher of Belmaduthy to keen-faced Mr. Mackenzie of Liverpool, one of the largest wool dealers and sheep buyers visiting the market. "You'll petter juist pe coming down to it at once." "I could not meet you at all." "I am afraid I'll pe doing what they'll pe laughing at me for." "We can't agree at all," are the words as a couple separate, probably to come together again later in the day. "An do reic thu na 'h'uainn fhathast. Coignasgailean?" "Cha neil fios again'm lieil thusa air son tavigse thoirtorra, Cnocnangraisheag?" "Thig gus ain fluich sin am bargan." Perhaps I had better translate. Two sheep-farmers are in colloquy, and address each other by the names of their farms, as is all but universal in the north. Cnocnangraisheag asks Coignasgailean, "Have you sold your lambs?" The cautious reply is, "I don't know; are you inclined to give me an offer?" and the proposal ensues. "Come and let us take a drink on the transaction." Let us follow the two worthies into the Caledonian. Jostling goes for nothing here, and you may shove as much in reason as you choose, taking your chance of reprisals from the sons of Anak. The lobbies of the Caledonian are full of men, drinking and bargaining with books in hand. There is no sitting room in all the house, and we follow the Cnocnangraisheag and his friend into the billiard room, where we are promptly served standing. What keenness of business-discussion mingled with what galore of whiskey there is everywhere! The whiskey seems to make no more impression than if it were ginger beer; and yet it is over-proof Talisker, as my throat and eyes find to their cost when I recklessly attempt to imitate Coignasgailean, and take a dram neat. As I pass the bar going out Willie Brown is bawling for soda with something in it, and Donald Murray of Geanies, one of the ablest men in the north of Scotland, brushes by with quick, decisive step. In the doorway stands the sturdy, square-built form of Macdonald of Balranald, the largest breeder of Highland cattle in

the country. Over the heathery pasture land of North
Uist 1,500 head and more of horned nowt of his range
in half-wild freedom. The Mundells and the Mitchells
seem ubiquitous. The ancestors of both families came
from England as shepherds when the Sutherland clear-
ances were made toward the end of last century, and
between them they now hold probably the largest acre-
age — or rather mileage, of sheep-farming territory in
all Scotland.

It is a "very dour market," that all admit. Everybody is holding back, for it is obvious prices are to be
"desperate high," and everybody wants to get the
full benefit of the rise. The pre-determination of the
Southern dealers to "buy out" freely at big prices
had been rashly revealed over-night by one of the fra-
ternity at the after-dinner toddy-symposium in the Caledonian. He had been sedulously plied with drink by
"Charlie Mitchell" and some others of the Ross and
Sutherland sheep-farmers, till reticence had departed
from his tongue. Ultimately he had leaped on the
table, breaking any quantity of glass-ware in the saltatory feat, and had asserted with free swearing his readiness to give 50s. all round for every three-year-old
wedder in the north of Scotland. His horror-stricken
partners rushed upon him, and bundled him downstairs
in hot haste, but the murder was out, and the "dour
market" was accounted for. Fancy 50s. a head for
beasts that do not weigh 60 lb. apiece as they come off
the hill! No wonder that we townsmen have to pay
dear for our mutton.

I push my way out of the heart of the market to
find the outlying neighborhood studded all over with
conversing groups. There is an all-pervading smell

of whiskey, and yet I see no man who has "turned a hair" by reason of the strength of the Talisker. A town-crier ringing a bell passes me. He halts, and the burden of his cry is, "There is a large supply of fresh haddies in the market!" The walls are placarded with advertisements of sheep smearing and dipping substances; the leading ingredients of which appear to be tar and butter. A recruiting sergeant of the Scots Fusilier Guards is standing by the Clachnacudden Stone, apparently in some dejection owing to the little business doing in his line. Men don't come to the "Character Fair" to 'list. It strikes me that quite three-fourths of the shops of Inverness are devoted to the sale of articles of Highland costume. Their fronts are hidden by hangings of tartan cloth; the windows are decked with sporrans, dirks, cairngorm plaid-brooches, ram's head snuff-boxes, bullocks' horns and skean dhus. If I chose I might enter the emporium of Messrs. Macdougall in my Sassenach garb and re-emerge in ten minutes outwardly a full-blown Highland chief, from the eagle's feather in my bonnet to the buckles on my brogues. Turning down High Street I reach the quay on the Ness bank, where I find in full blast a horse fair of a very miscellaneous description, and totally destitute of the features that have earned for the wool market the title of "Character Fair." There are blood colts running chiefly to stomach, splints and bog spavins; ponies with shaggy manes, trim barrels, and clean legs; and slack-jointed cart horses, nearly asleep — for "ginger" is an institution which does not seem to have come so far north as Inverness. Business is lively here, the chronic "dourness" of a market being discounted by the scarcity of horseflesh.

At four o'clock we sit down to the market ordinary in the great room of the Caledonian. A member of Parliament occupies the chair, one of the croupiers is a baronet, the other the chief of the clan Mackintosh. There is a great collection of north-country notabilities, and tables upon tables of sheep-farmers and sheep-dealers. We have a considerable *cacoethes* of speech-making, among the orators being Professor Blackie of Edinburgh, whose quaint comicalities convulse his audience. It is pretty late when the Professor rises to speak, and the whiskey has been flowing free. Some one interjects a whiskeyfied interruption into the Professor's speech, who at once in stentorian tones issues orders that the disturber of the harmony of the evening shall be summarily consigned to the lunatic asylum. I see him ejected with something like the force of a stone from a catapult, and have no reasonable doubt that he will spend the night an inmate of "Craig Duncan." The speeches over, bargaining recommences moistened by toddy, which fluid appears to exercise an appreciable softening influence on the "dourness" of the market. Till long after midnight seasoned vessels are talking and dealing, booking sales while they sip their tenth tumbler.

I have to leave on the Saturday morning, but I make no doubt that the skeleton programme given at the beginning of this paper will have its bones duly clothed with flesh.

MISS PRIEST'S BRIDECAKE.

In broad essentials the marryings and givings in marriage of India now-a-days do not greatly differ from these natural phenomena at home; but to use a florist's phrase they are more inclined to "sport." The old days are over when consignments of damsels were made to the Indian marriage-market, in the assured certainty that the young ladies would be brides-elect before reaching the landing ghât. The increased facilities which improved means of transit now offer to bachelors for running home on short leave have resulted in making the Anglo-Indian "spin" rather a drug in the market; and operating in the same untoward direction is the growing predilection on the part of the Anglo-Indian bachelor for other men's wives, in preference to hampering himself with the encumbrance of a wife of his own. Among other social products of India old maids are now occasionally found; and the fair creature who on her first arrival would smile only on commissioners or colonels has been fain, after a few — yet too many — hot seasons have impaired her bloom and lowered her pretensions, to put up with a lieutenant or even with a dissenting *padre*. Slips between the cup and the lip are more frequent in India than in England. Loving and riding away is not wholly unknown in the Anglo-Indian community; and indeed, by both parties to the contract, engagements are frequently regarded in the mistaken light of ninepins. Hearts are seldom broken. At Simla during a late season a gallant captain persistently wore the willow till the war broke out, because he had been jilted in favor of a colonel; but his appetite rapidly recovered its tone on campaign, and he was reported to have re-opened relations by correspondence from the tented field with a former object of his affections. Not long ago there arrived in an up-country station a box containing a wedding-trousseau, which a lady had ordered out from home as the result of an engagement between her and a gallant warrior. But in the interval the warrior had departed elsewhere, and had addressed to the lady a pleasant and affable communication, setting forth that there was insanity in his family, and that he must have been laboring under an access of the family disorder when he had proposed to her. It was hard to get such a letter, and it must have been harder still for her to gaze on the abortive wedding-dress. But the lady did not abandon herself to despair; she took a practical view of the situation. She determined to keep the trousseau by her for six months in case she might within that time achieve a fresh conquest, when it would come in happily. Should fortune not favor her thus far, she meant to advertise the wedding-gear for sale.

Miss Priest was no " spin " lingering on in spinsterhood against her will. It is true that when I saw her first she had already been " out " three years, but she might have been married a dozen times over had she chosen. I have seen many pretty faces in the fair Anglo-Indian sisterhood, but Miss Priest had a brightness and a sparkle that were all her own. At flirting, at riding, at walking, at dancing, at performing in amateur theatricals, at making fools of men in an airy, ruthless, good-hearted fashion, Miss Priest, as an old soldier might say, "took the right of the line." There was a fresh vitality about the girl that drew men and women alike to her. You met her at dawn cantering round Jakko on her pony. Before breakfast she had been rinking for an hour, with as likely as not a waltz or two thrown in. She never missed a picnic to Annandale, the Waterfalls, or Mashobra. Another turn at the Benmore rink before dinner, and for sure a dance after, rounded off this young lady's normal day during the Simla season. But if pleasure-loving, capricious, and reckless, she scraped through the ordeal of Simla gossip without incurring scandal. She was such a frank honest girl that malign tongues might assail her indeed, but ineffectually. And she had given proof that she knew how to take care of herself, although her only protectress was a perfectly inoffensive mother. On the occasion of the Prince of Wales's visit to Lahore, had she not boxed the ears of a burly and somewhat boorish swain, who had chosen the outside of an elephant as an eligible *locale* for a proposal, the uncouth abruptness of which did not accord with her notions of the fitness of things?

Miss Priest may be said to have lived in a chronic state of engagements. The engagements never seemed to come to any thing, but that was on account mostly of the young lady's wilfulness. It bothered her to be engaged to the same man for more than from a week to ten days on end. No bones were broken; the gentlemen resigned the position at her behest, and she would genially dance with them the same night.

Malice and heart-burning were out of the question with a lissom, winsome, witching fairy like this, who played with her life as a child does with soap-bubbles, and who was as elusory and irresponsible as a summer-day rainbow. But one season at Mussoorie Miss Priest contracted an engagement somewhat less evanescent. Mussoorie is, of all the Himalayan hill-stations, the most demure and proper. Simla occasionally is convulsed by scandals, although dispassionate inquiry invariably proves that there is nothing in them. The hot blood of the quick and fervid Punjaub — casual observers have called the Punjaub stupid, but the remark applies only to its officials — is apt to stir the current of life at Murree. The chiefs of the North-West are invariably so intolerably proper that occasional revolt from their austerity is all but forced on Nynee Tal, the sanatorium of that province. But Mussoorie, undisturbed by the presence of frolicsome viceroys or austere lieutenant-governors, is a limpid pool of pleasant propriety. It is not so much that it is decorous as that it is genuinely good; it is a favorite resort of clergymen and of clergymen's wives. It was at Mussoorie that Miss Priest met Captain Hambleton, a gallant gunner. They danced together at the Assembly Rooms; they rode in company round the Camel's Back; they went to the same picnics at "The Glen." The captain proposed and was accepted. For about the nineteenth time Miss Priest was an engaged young lady. And Captain Hambleton was a lover of rather a different stamp from the men with whom her name previously had been nominally coupled. He was in love and he was a gentleman; he had proposed to the girl, not that he and she should be merely engaged, but that they should be married also. This view of the subject was novel to Miss Priest, and at first she thought it rather a bore; but the captain pegged away, and gradually the lady came rather to relish the situation. Men and women concurred that the wayward pinions of the fair Bella were at last trimmed if not clipped; and to do her justice, the general opinion was that, once married, she would make an excellent wife. As the close of the Mussoorie season approached, the invitations went out for Bella Priest's wedding, and for " cake and wine afterwards at the house." The wedding-breakfast is a comparatively rare *tamasha* in India; the above is the formula of the usual invitation at the hill-stations.

It happened that just two days before the day fixed for the marriage of Miss Priest and Captain Hambleton, there was a fancy-dress ball in the Assembly Rooms at Mussoorie. I think that as a rule fancy-dress balls are greater successes in India than at home. People in India give their minds more to the selection and to the elaboration of costumes; and there is less of that *mauvaise honte* when masquerading in fancy costume which makes a ball of this description at home so wooden and wanting in go. At a fancy ball in India " the Devil " acts accordingly, and manages his tail with adroitness and grace. It is a fact that at a recent fancy-dress ball in Lahore, a game was played on the lap of a lady who appeared as " chess," with the chessmen which had formed her head-dress. This Mussoorie ball, being the last of the season, was to excel all its predecessors in inventive variety. A *padre's* wife conceived the bright idea of appearing as Eve; and only abandoned the notion on finding that no matter what species of thread she used, it tore the fig-leaves; a result which, besides causing her a disappointment, imperilled her immortal soul by engendering doubts as to the truth of the scriptural narrative of the creation. Miss Priest determined to go to this ball, although doing so under the circumstances was scarcely in accordance with the *convenances;* but Miss Priest had never cared particularly much about the *convenances*, and she was a girl very much addicted to having her own way. Captain Hambleton did not wish her to go, and there was a temporary coolness between the two on the subject; but he yielded and they made it up. The principle as to her going once established, Miss Priest's next task was to set about the invention of a costume. It was to be her last effort as a "spin;" and she determined it should be worthy of her reputation for brilliant inventiveness. She had shone as a Vivandière, as the Daughter of the Regiment, as a Greek Slave, Grace Darling, and so forth, times out of number; but these characters were stale. Miss Priest had a form of supple rounded grace, nor had Diana shapelier limbs. A great inspiration came to her as she sauntered pondering on the Mall. Let her go as Ariel, all gauze, flesh-tints, and natural curves! She hailed the happy thought, and invested in countless yards of gauze. She had the tights already by her.

Now Miss Priest, knowing the idiosyncrasy of Captain Hambleton, had little doubt that he would put his foot down upon Ariel. But she knew he loved her, and with characteristic recklessness determined to trust to that and to luck. She too loved him, even better, perhaps, than Ariel; but she hoped to keep both the captain and the character. She did not, however, tell him of her design, waiting perhaps for a favorable opportunity. But even in Arcadian Mussoorie there are the " d——d good-natured friends " of whom Byron wrote ; and one of these — of course it was a woman — told Captain Hambleton of the character in which Miss Priest intended to appear at the fancy ball. The captain was a headstrong sort of man — what in India is called *zubburdustee*. Instead of calling on the girl, and talking to her as a wise man would have done, he sat down and wrote her a terse letter, forbidding her to appear as Ariel, and adding that if she should persist in doing so, their engagement must be considered at an end. Miss Priest naturally fired up. Strangely enough. being a woman, she did not reply to the captain's letter ; but when the evening of the ball came, duly appeared as Ariel, with rather less gauze about her shapely limbs than had been her original intention. She created an immense sensation. Some of the ladies frowned, others turned up their noses, yet others tucked in their skirts when she approached ; and all vowed that they would decline to touch Miss Priest's hand in the quadrille. Miss Priest did not care a jot for these demonstrations. and she never danced square dances. Among the gentlemen she created a perfect furore.

Captain Hambleton was present at the ball. For the greater part of the evening he stood near the door with his eye fixed on Miss Priest, apparently rather in sorrow than in anger. His gaze seemed but to stimulate her to more vivacious flirtation, and she " carried on above a bit," as a cynical subaltern remarked, with the gallant major to whom she had been penultimately engaged. Toward the close of the evening Captain Hambleton relinquished his post of observation, seemed to accept the situation, and was observed at supper-time paying marked attention to a married lady with whom his name had been to some extent coupled not long before his engagement to Miss Priest.

Next morning Miss Priest took time by the forelock. She waited for no further communication from Captain Hambleton; he had already sent his ultimatum, and she had dared her fate. The morrow was the day fixed for the marriage. Many people had been bidden. Mussoorie, including Landour, is a large station, and the postal delivery of letters is not particularly punctual. So she adopted a plan for warning off the wedding-guests identical with that employed in Indian stations for circulating notifications as to lawn-tennis gatherings and unimportant intimations generally. At the head of the paper is written the notification, underneath are the names of the persons concerned. The document is intrusted to a messenger known as a *chuprassee*, who goes away on his circuit; and each person writes " Seen " opposite his or her name in testimony of being posted in the intelligence conveyed in the notification. Miss Priest divided the invited guests into four rounds, and despatched four *chuprassees*, each bearing a document curtly announcing that " Miss Priest's marriage will not come off as arranged, and the invitations therefore are to be regarded as cancelled."

Miss Priest had no fortune, and her mother was by no means wealthy. It may seem strange to English readers — not nearly so much so, however, as to Anglo-Indians ones — that Captain Hambleton had thought it a graceful and kindly attention to provide the wedding-cake. It had reached him across the hills from Peliti's the night of the ball, and now here it was on his hands — a great white elephant. Whether in the hope that it might be regarded as an olive-branch, whether that he burned to be rid of it somehow, or whether, knowing that Miss Priest was bound to get married some day, and thinking that it would be a convenience if she had a bridecake by her handy for the occasion, there is no evidence. Anyhow, he sent it to Mrs. Priest with his compliments. That very sensible woman did not send it back with a cutting message, as some people would have done. Having considerable Indian experience, she had learned practical wisdom, and the short-sighted folly of cutting messages. She kept the bridecake, and enclosed to the gallant captain Gosslett's bill for the dozen of simkin that excellent firm had sent in to wash it down wherewithal.

Bridecakes are bores to carry about from place to place, and Miss Priest and her mother were rather birds of passage. Peliti declined to take this particular bridecake back, for all Simla had seen it in his window, and he saw no possibility of "working it in." So the Priests, mother and daughter, determined to realize on it in a somewhat original and indeed cynical fashion. The cake was put up to be raffled for.

All the station took tickets for the fun of the thing. Captain Hambleton was anxious to show that there was no ill-feeling, and did not find himself so unhappy as he had expected — perhaps from the *redintegratio amoris* in another quarter; so he took his ticket in the raffle like other people. It is needless to say that he won; and the cake duly came back to him.

Had Captain Hambleton been a superstitious man he might have regarded this strange occurrence as indicating that the Fates willed it that he should compass somehow a union with Miss Priest. But the captain had no superstition in his nature; and, indeed, had begun to think that he was well out of it; besides which it was currently reported that Miss Priest had already re-engaged herself to another man. But the bridecake was upon him as the Philistines upon Samson; and the question was, what the devil to do with it? He couldn't raffle it over again; nobody would take tickets. He had half a mind to trundle it over the *khud* (*Anglicè*, precipice) and be done with it; but then again he reflected that this would be sheer waste, and might seem to indicate soreness on his part. It cost him a good many pegs before he thought the matter out in all its bearings, for, as has been said, he was a gunner; but as he sauntered away from the club in the small hours a happy thought came to him.

He would give a picnic, at which the bogey bridecake should figure conspicuously, and then be laid finally by the process of demolition. His leave was nearly up; he had experienced much hospitality, and a picnic would be a graceful and genial acknowledgment thereof. And he would ask the Priests, just like other people, and no doubt they would enter into the spirit of the thing and not send a "decline." Bella, he knew, liked picnics nearly as well as balls, and it must be a powerful reason indeed that would keep her away from either.

Captain Hambleton's picnic was the last of the season, and everybody called it the brightest. "The Glen" resounded to the laughter at tiffin, and the shades of night were falling ere stray couples turned up from its more sequestered recesses. Amid loud cheers Miss Priest, although still Miss Priest, cut up her own bridecake with a serene equanimity that proved the charming sweetness of her disposition. There was no marriage-bell, yet all went merry as a marriage-bell, which is occasionally rather a sombre tintinnabulation; and the *débris* of the bridecake finally fell to the sweeper.

I would fain that it were possible, having a regard to truth, to round off this little story prettily by telling how, in a glade of "The Glen," after the demolition of the bridecake, Miss Priest and the captain "squared matters," were duly married, and lived happily ever after, as the story-books say. But this consummation was not attained. Miss Priest indeed was in the glade, but it was not with the captain, or at least this particular captain; and as for him, he spent the afternoon placidly smoking cigarettes, as he lay at the feet of his married consoler. To the best of my knowledge Miss Priest is Miss Priest still.

THE CAWNPORE OF TO-DAY.

The traveller up the country from Calcutta does not speedily reach places the names of which vividly recall the episodes of the great mutiny. It is a chance, if, as the train passes Dinapore, he remembers the defection of the brigade stationed there whom Koer Singh seduced from their allegiance. Arrah may possibly recall a dim memory of Wake's splendid defence of Boyle's bungalow, and of Vincent Eyre's dashingly-executed relief of the indomitable garrison. Benares is off the main line — on whose parade-ground Neill first put down that peremptory foot of his, where Olpherts was so quick with those guns of his, and Jim Elliot did his grim work with noose and cross-beam until long after the going down of the summer sun. But when the traveller's eye first rests on the gray ramparts of Akbar's hoary fortress, in the angle where the Ganges and the Jumna meet and blend one with another, the reality of the mutiny begins to impress itself upon him. Allahabad was the scene of a terrible tragedy; it was the point of departure also whence Havelock set forward on Cawnpore with his column, not, indeed of rescue, but of retribution. The journey from Allahabad to Cawnpore, although performed in the night, is not one to be slept through by any student of the story of the great rebellion. The Indian moon pours her flood of light on the little knoll hard by Futtehpore, where Havelock stood when Jwala Pershad's first round shot came lobbing through his staff in among the camp kettles of the 64th. That village beyond the mango tope is Futtehpore itself, whence the rebel sowars swept headlong down the *chaussée*, till Maude's guns gave them the word to halt. The pools are dry now through which, when Hamilton's voice had rung out the " Forward — at the double ! " the light company of the Ross-shire Buffs splashed recklessly past the abandoned sepoy guns, in their race with the grenadier company of the 64th, that had for its goal the Pandy barricade outside the village. In that cluster of mud huts — its name is Aoong — the gallant Renaud fell with a shattered thigh, as he led his " Lambs " up to the *épaulement* which covered its front. One fight a day is fair allowance anywhere, but those fellows whom Havelock led were gluttons for fighting. Spanning that deep rugged nullah there, down which the Pandoo flows turbulently in the rainy season, is the bridge across which, in the afternoon of the morning of Aoong, Stephenson, with his Fusiliers, dashed into the sepoy battery, and bayoneted the gunners before they could make up their minds to run away. And it was in the gray morning following the day of that double battle (the 15th of July) that the general, having heard for the first time that there were still alive in Cawnpore a number of women and children who had escaped the massacre of the boats, told his men what he knew. " With God's help," shouted Havelock, with a break in the loud voice that was like a sob, as he stood with his hat off and his hand on his sword, " with God's help, men, we will save them, or every man die in the attempt." One answer came back in a great cheer; but a sadder answer to the aspiration, a bitter truth that made that aspiration futile and hopeless, had lain ever since the evening of the day before in the Beebeegur, and almost as the chief was speaking the Well was receiving its dead inmates. Where the train begins to slacken its pace on approaching the station, it is passing over the field of the first — the creditable — battle of Cawnpore. Fresh from the butchery Dhoondoo Punth himself had come out to aid in the last stand against the avengers. Yonder is the mango tope which formed the screen for Walter Hamilton's turning movement. It needs little imagination to recall the scene. Close by, at the cross roads, stands the sepoy battery, and these horsemen still nearer are reconnoitring sowars. Beyond the road the Highlanders are deploying on the plain, as they clear the sheltering flank of the mango trees, amidst a grim silence, broken only by the crash of the bursting shells and the cries of the bullock drivers as the guns rattle on to open fire from the reverse flank. The flush rises in Hamilton's face, and the eyes of him begin to sparkle as he shouts, " Ross-shire Buffs, wheel into line," and then " Forward." Quick as lightning the trails of the sepoy guns are swung round, and shot and shell come crashing through the ranks, while the rebel infantry, with a swiftness which speaks well for their British drill, show a front against this inroad on their flank. With silent, grim imperturbability, the Highland line stalks steadily on with the long, springy step to be learned only on the heather. Now they are within eighty yards of the muzzles of the guns, and they can see the color of the mustaches of the men plying and supporting them. Then Hamilton, with his sword in the air, and his face all ablaze with the fighting blood in him, turns round in the saddle, shouts "Charge!" and bids the pipers to strike up. Wild and shrill bursts over that Indian plain the rude notes of the northern music. But louder yet, drowning them and the roll of the artillery, rings out that Highland warcry that has so often presaged victory to British arms. The Ross-shire men are in and over the guns ere even the gunners have time to drop their lint-stocks and ramming-rods; they fall upon the supporting infantry, with their bayonets at the charge, and the supporting infantry go down where they huddle together, lacking the opportunity to break and run away in time. But the battle rages all day, and the white soldiers, as they fight their way slowly forward, hear the bursts of military music that greet the Nana as he moves from place to place, *not* in the immediate front. Barrow and his eighteen cavalry volunteers crash into the thick of them, with the informal order to his men, "Give point, lads; damn cuts and guards." Young Havelock, mounted by the side of the gallant and ill-fated Stirling, trudging forward on foot, brings the 64th on at the double against the great 24-pounder on the Cawnpore road that is vomiting grape at point-blank range. The night falls and the battle ceases; but among the wearied fighting men there is none of the elation of victory, for through the ranks, after the going down of the sun, had throbbed the bruit, originating no one knew where, that the women and children in Cawnpore had been butchered on the afternoon of the day before, while Stephenson and his Fusiliers were carrying the bridge of the Pandoo Nuddee.

The railway station of Cawnpore is distant more

than a mile from the cantonment. Close to the road, and not far from the station, the explorer easily finds the massive pile of the "Savada House," now allotted as residences for railway officials. English children play now in the corridors once thronged by the minions of the Nana, for here were his headquarters during most of the siege. Its verandas all day long were full of ministers, diviners, courtiers, and creatures. Here strolled the supple, panther-like Azimoolah — the self-asserted favorite of home society in the pre-Mutiny days. Teeka Sing, the Nana's war minister, had his "bureau" in a tent under the peepul tree there. In that other clump of trees, where an ayah is tickling a white baby into laughter, was the pavilion of the Nana himself, who inherited the Mahratta preference for canvas over bricks and mortar. And here, while the crackle of the musketry fire and the din of the big guns came softened on the ear by distance, sat the adopted son of the Peishwa, while Jwala Pershad came for orders about the cavalry, and Bala Rao, his brother, explained his devices for harassing the sahibs, and Tantia Topee, Hoolass Sing, Azimoolah, and the Nana himself devised the scheme of the treachery. But the Savada House has even a more lurid interest than this. Hither the women and children, whom an unkind fate had spared from dying with the men, were brought back from the Ghaut of Slaughter. You may see the two rooms into which a hundred and twenty-five were huddled after that march from before the presence of one death into the presence of another. As they plodded past the intrenchment so long held, and across the plain to the Nana's pavilion, "I saw," says a spectator, "that many of the ladies were wounded.

Their clothes had blood upon them. Two were badly hurt and had their heads bound up with handkerchiefs, some were wet, covered with mud and blood, and some had their dresses torn, but all had clothes. I saw one or two children without clothes. There were no men in the party, but only some boys of 12 or 13. Some of the ladies were barefoot." Hither, too, were sent later the women of that detachment of the garrison that had been got off from the ghaut in the boat defended by Vibart, Ashe, Delafosse, Bolton, Moore, and Thomson, and that had been captured at Nuzzufghur by Baboo Ram Bux. It had been for these people a turbulent departure from the Suttee Chowra Ghaut, but it was a yet more fearful returning. "They were brought back," testified a spy, "60 sahibs, 25 mem sahibs, and four children. The Nana ordered the sahibs to be separated from the mem sahibs, and shot by the 1st Bengal Native Infantry. . . . 'Then,' said one of the mem sahibs, 'I will not leave my husband. If he must die I will die with him.' So she ran and sat down behind her husband, clasping him round the waist. Directly she said this, the other mem sahibs said, 'We also will die with our husbands,' and they all sat down each by her husband. Then their husbands said, 'Go back,' but they would not. Whereupon the Nana ordered his soldiers, and they go in, pulling them forcibly away." . . .

The drive from the railway station to the European cantonments is pleasant and shaded. At a bend in the road there comes into view a broad, flat, treeless parade-ground. This plain lies within a circle of foliage, above which, on the south-eastern side, rise the balconies and flat tops of a long range of barracks built in detached blocks, while around the rest of the circle the trees shade the bungalows of the cantonment. Near the centre of this level space there is an irregular enclosure defined by a shallow sunk wall and low quickset hedge, and in the middle of this enclosure rises the ornate and not wholly satisfactory structure known as the "Memorial Church." It is built on the site of the old dragoon hospital, which was the very focus of the agony of the siege. It is impossible to analyze the mingled emotions of amazement, pride, pity, wrath, and sorrow which filled the visitor to the shrine of British valor, endurance, and constancy. The heart swells and the eyes fill as one, standing here with all the theatre of the heroism lying under one's eyes, recalls the episodes of the glorious, piteous story. The blood stirs when one remembers the buoyant valor of the gallant Moore, who "wherever he passed left men something more courageous and women something less unhappy," of the reckless audacity of Ashe, the cool daring of Delafosse, the deadly rifle of Stirling, the heroic devotion of Jervis. And a great lump grows in the throat when one bethinks him of the beautiful constancy and fearful sufferings of the women; of British ladies going barefoot and giving up their stockings as cases for grapeshot; of Mrs. Moore's journeys across to No. 2 Barracks; of the hapless gentlewomen, "unshod, unkempt, ragged, and squalid, haggard and emaciated, parched with drought, and faint with hunger, sitting waiting to hear that they were widows." And what a place it was which the garrison had to defend! Not a foot of all the space bomb-proof, the apology for an intrenchment, such as "an active cow might jump over." The imagination has to do much work here, for most of the landmarks are gone. The outline of the world-famous earthwork is almost wholly obliterated; only in places is it to be dimly recognized by brick-discolored lines, and a low raised line on the smooth maidan. The enclosure now existing has no reference to the outlines of the intrenchment. That enclosure merely surrounds the graveyard, in the midst of which stands the "Memorial Church," a structure that cannot be commended from an architectural point of view. But the space enclosed around its gaunt red walls is pregnant with painful interest. We come first on a railed-in memorial tomb, bearing an inscription in raised letters, on a cross let into the tessellated pavement: "In three graves within this enclosure lie the remains of Major Edward Vibart, 2nd Bengal Cavalry, and about seventy officers and soldiers, who, after escaping from the massacre at Cawnpore, on the 27th June, 1857, were captured by the rebels at Sheorapore, and murdered on the 1st July." The inmates of these graves were originally buried elsewhere, and were removed hither when the enclosure was formed. In another part of the enclosure is a raised tomb, the slab of which bears the inscription: "This stone marks a spot which lay within Wheeler's intrenchment, and covers the remains and is sacred to the memory of those who were the first to meet their death when beleaguered by mutineers and rebels in June, 1857." Two only lie in this grave, Mr. Murphy and a lady who died of fever. These two perished on the first day of the siege, and had the exclusive privilege of being decently interred within the precincts of the intrenchment. After the first day of the siege there was scant leisure for funeral rites. To find the last resting-place of the remaining dead of this siege we must quit the enclosure and walk across the maidan to a spot among the trees by the roadside under the shadow of No. 4 Barrack. There was an empty well here when the siege begun; three weeks after, when the siege ended, this well contained the bodies of 250 British people. With daylight the battle raged around that sepulchre, but when the night came the slain of the day were borne thither with stealthy step and scant attendance. Now the well is filled up, and above it, inside a small, ornamental enclosure, formed by iron railings, there rises a monument which bears the following inscription: "In a well under this enclosure were laid by the hands of their fellows in suffering the bodies of men, women, and children, who died hard by during the heroic defence of Wheeler's intrenchment when beleaguered by the rebel Nana." Below the inscription is this apposite quotation from Psalm cxli.: "Our bones are scattered at the grave's mouth, as when one cutteth and cleaveth wood upon the earth. But mine eyes are unto Thee, O God the Lord." At the corners of the flower-plot are small crosses bearing individual names. One commemorates Sir George Parker, the cantonment magistrate; a second, Captain Jenkins; a third, Lieutenant Saunders and the men of the 84th Regiment; a fourth, Lieutenant Glanville and the men of the Madras Fusiliers; and here, too, lies stout-hearted yet tender-hearted John MacKillop of the Civil Service, the hero of another well — that from which the team of buffaloes are now drawing water to make the mortar for the Memorial Church. Thence was procured the water for the garrison, and it was a target also for the rebel artillery, so that the appearance of a man with a pitcher by day, and by night the creaking of the tackle, was the signal for a shower of grape. But John MacKillop, "not being a fighting man," made himself useful, as he modestly put it, for a week as Captain of the Well, till a grapeshot sent him to that other well thence never to return.

The Memorial Church is in the form of a cross, and now that it is at last finished, is not destitute of beauty as regards its interior. Perhaps it is in place, but the noblest monument that could commemorate Cawnpore would have the maintenance, for the wonder of the world unto all time, of the intrenchment and what it surrounded, as nearly as possible in the condition in which they were left on the evacuation of the garrison. The grandest monument in the world is the residency of Lucknow, which remains and is kept up substantially in the condition in which it was left when Sir Colin Campbell brought out its garrison in November, 1857; and the Cawnpore intrenchment would have been a still nobler memorial, as the abiding testimony to a defence even more wonderful, although unfortunately unsuccessful, than that of Lucknow. But the Memorial Church of Cawnpore will always be interesting by reason of its site, and of the memorial tablets on the walls of its interior. In the left transept is a tablet "To the memory of the Engineers of the East Indian Railway, who died and were killed in the great insurrection of 1857; erected in affectionate remembrance by their brother Engineers in the North-West Provinces." On the left side of the nave are several tablets. One is to the memory of poor young

John Nicklen Martin, killed in the boats at Suttee Chowra Ghaut. Another commemorates three officers, two sergeants, two corporals, a drummer, and twenty privates of the 34th Regiment killed at the (second) Battle of Cawnpore, on the 28th November, 1857; the day on which the Gwalior contingent, seduced into rebellion by Tantia Topee, made itself so unpleasant to General Windham, the "Cawnpore Runners," and other regiments of that officer's command. A third is "To the memory of E. G. Chalwin, 2nd Light Cavalry, and his wife Louisa, who both perished during the siege of Cawnpore in July, 1857. These are they which came out of great tribulation." A fourth commemorates Captain Gordon and Lieutenant Hensley, of the 82nd Foot, also victims of the Gwalior contingent. In the right of the nave there is a tablet "Sacred to the memory of Philip Hayes Jackson, who, with Jane, his wife, and her brother, Ralf Blyth Croker, were massacred by rebels at Cawnpore on 27th June." Another is to Lieutenant Angelo, of 16th Grenadiers Bengal Native Infantry, who also fell in the boat massacre; and a third is to the memory of the gallant Stuart Beatson, who was Havelock's adjutant-general, and who, dying as he was of cholera, did his work at Pandoo Nuddee and Cawnpore in a dhoolie. In the right transept are tablets in memory of the officers of the Connaught Rangers, and of the officers and men of the 32nd Cornwall Regiment, "who fell in defence of Lucknow and Cawnpore and subsequent campaign" — 14 officers and 448 "women and men." And here, too, is perhaps the most affecting memorial of any — a tablet "In memory of Mrs. Moore, Mrs. Wainwright, Miss Wainwright, Mrs. Hill, 43 soldiers' wives, and 55 children, murdered in Cawnpore in June, 1857."

It is easy enough now to follow the footsteps of Mrs. Moore, dangerous as was that journey of hers, from the intrenchment to the corner of No. 2 Barrack, which she was wont to make when her husband went on duty there to strengthen the hands of Mowbray Thomson. There is no trace now, and the very memory of its whereabouts is lost, of the bamboo hut in a sheltered corner which the garrison of this exposed post built for the brave gentlewoman. But No. 2 Barrack, except that it is finished and tenanted, stands now very much as it did when Glanville first, and when he fell then Mowbray Thomson, defended with a success which seems so wonderful when we look at the place defended and its situation. The garrison was not always the same. "My sixteen men," writes Thomson, "consisted in the first instance of Ensign Henderson, of the 56th Native Infantry, five or six of the Madras Fusiliers; two plate-layers and some men of the 84th. The first instalment was soon disabled. The Madras Fusiliers were all shot at their posts. Several of the 84th also fell, but in consequence of the importance of the position, as soon as a loss in my little corps was reported, Captain Moore sent us over a re-enforcement from the intrenchment. Sometimes a soldier, sometimes a civilian, came. The orders given us were not to surrender with our lives. and we did our best to obey them." And in a line with No. 2 Barrack is No. 4 Barrack, held with equal stanchness by a party of civil engineers who had been employed on the East Indian Railroad, and who had for their commander Captain Jenkins. Seven of the engineers perished in the defence of this post.

There is nothing more to see on the maidan, and one

feels his anger rising at the obliteration of every thing that might help toward the localization of associations. Let us leave the scene of the defence, and follow the track of the defenders as they marched down to the scene of the great treachery. The distance from the intrenchment to the ghaut is barely a mile. Think of that stirrup-cup — that *doch an dhorras* — of cold water, in which the hapless band pledged one another. The noble Moore cheerily leads the way down the slope to the bridge with the white rails with an advance guard of a handful of his 32nd men. The palanquins with the women, the children, and the wounded follow, the latter bandaged up with strips of women's gowns and petticoats, and fragments of shirt-sleeves. And then come the fighting men — a gallant, ragged, indomitable band. A martinet colonel would stand aghast — for save for a regimental button here and there, he would find it hard to recognize the gaunt, hairy, sun-scorched squad for British soldiers. But let who might incline to disown these few war-worn men in their dirty flannel rags and fragmentary nankeen breeches, their foes know them for what they are, and make way for the white sahibs, with no dressing indeed in their ranks, but each man with his rifle on his shoulder, the deadly revolver in his belt, and the fearless glance in the hollow eye. The wooden bridge with the white rails spans at right angles a rough irregular glen, which widens out as it approaches the river, some three hundred yards distant from the bridge. It is a mere footpath that leaves the road on the hither side of the bridge, and skirting the dry bed of the nullah, touches the river close to the old temple. By this footpath it was that our countrymen and countrywomen passed down to the trap that had been laid for them in the mouth of the glen. There are few to whom the details of that fell scene are not familiar. What a contrast between the turmoil and devilry of it, and the serene calmness of the all but solitude the Ghaut now presents! On the knolls of the further side snug bungalows nestle among the trees, under the veranda of one of which a lady is playing with her children. The village of Suttee Chowra on the bluff on the left of the Ghaut, where Tantia Topee's sepoys were concealed, no longer exists; a pretty bungalow and its compound occupy its site. The little temple on the water's edge by the Ghaut is slowly mouldering into decay; on the plaster of the coping of its river wall you may see the marks of the treacherous bullets. The stair which, built against its wall, led down to the water's edge, has disappeared. Tantia Topee's dispositions for the perpetration of the treachery could not now succeed, for the Ganges has changed its course, and there is deep water close in shore at the Ghaut. In the stream nearest to the Oude side the river has cast up a long narrow dearah island, in the fertile mud of which melons are cultivated where once whistled the shot from the guns on the Oude side of the river. A Brahmin priest is placidly sunning himself on the river platform of the temple, over the dome of which hangs the foliage of a peepul tree. A dhobie is washing the shirts of a sahib in the stream that once was dyed with the blood of the sahibs. There is no monument here, no superfluous reminder of the terrible tragedy. The man is not to be envied whose eyes are dry, and whose heart beats its normal pulsations, while he stands here alone in this spot so densely peopled by associations at once so tragic and so glorious.

The scene of the massacre lies some distance higher up the river. As we cross the Ganges Canal, the native city lying on our left, there rises up before us the rich mass of foliage that forms the outer screen of the beautiful Memorial Gardens. The hue of the greenery would be sombre but for the blossoms which relieve it, emblem of the divine hope which mitigated the gloom of despair for our countrywomen who perished so cruelly in this balefully historic spot. Of the Beebeeghur, the term by which among the natives is known the bungalow where the massacre was perpetrated, not one stone now remains on another, but neither its memory nor its name will be lost for all time. Natives are strolling in the shady flower-bordered walks of the Memorial Gardens, the prohibition which long debarred their entrance having been wisely removed. In the centre of the garden rises, fringed with cypresses, a low mound, the summit of which is crowned by a circular screen, or border, of light and beautiful open-work architecture. The circular space enclosed is sunk, and from the centre of this sunk space there rises a pedestal on which stands the marble presentment of an angel. There is no need to explain what episode in the tragic store this monument commemorates; the inscription round the capital of the pedestal tells its tale succinctly indeed, but the words burn. "Sacred," it runs, "to the perpetual memory of the great company of Christian people, chiefly women and children, who near this spot were cruelly massacred by the followers of the rebel Nana Doondoo Punth of Bithoor; and cast, the dying with the dead, into the well below, on the 15th day of July, 1857." A few paces to the north-west of the monument is the spot where stood the bungalow in which the massacre was done ; and now, where the sight they saw maddened our countrymen long ago to a frenzy of revenge, there bloom roses and violets. And a step further on, in a thicket of *arbor vitæ* trees and cypresses, is the "Memorial Churchyard," with its many nameless mounds, for here were buried not a few who died during the long occupation of Cawnpore, and in the combats around it. Here there is a monument to Thornhill, the judge of Futtehghur, Mary his wife, and their two children, who perished in the massacre. Thornhill was one of the males brought out from the bungalow and shot earlier in the afternoon than the women's time came. Another monument bears this inscription : — " Sacred to the memory of the women and children of the 32nd, this monument is raised by twenty men of the same regiment, who were passing through Cawnpore, Nov. 21, 1857." An officer who formerly belonged to the company lays a stone to the memory of the women and children of the 1st Company 61st Bengal Native Infantry, and among the tombstones are those of gallant Douglas Campbell of the 78th, Woodford of the 2nd Battalion Rifle Brigade, and Young of the 4th Bengal Native Infantry.

CHRISTMAS PRESENTS BY POST.

Six o'clock has struck at St. Martin's-le-Grand. The letter and newspaper traps have shut with an inexorable bang. The yard is crowded with mail carts, and the crowd is swollen by other carts which come trooping in from the district stations. Porters are swarming from the carts to the shoots, staggering under great sacks, of which they rid themselves with a grunt such as a pavier emits as his blow descends. We enter the building, and, threading innumerable passages, step out on to the balcony that overhangs and overlooks the great hall, or rather series of halls, of the Circulation Department. "I stood on the bridge" — not indeed at midnight, nor "heard the breakers roar;" but heard instead a continuous pattering of stamping like the steady rattle of a hailstorm on a wooden roof. At one set of tables boys are "facing" the letters — placing them right end up, in order to be dealt with by the nimble-wristed men who are plying the stamping instruments with a deft celerity that only long practice could impart. There are pyramids of letters here, but no sacks; for this is the East Central Department, where are dealt with letters posted at St. Martin's-le-Grand itself, and from the wells underneath the shoots the letters are brought in baskets to the "facing" tables. It is not here, but in another division of the huge open space, where the letters are sorted and disposed of, that we saw being brought in from the district post-offices in the mail-carts. This latter hall, as we look down upon it, seems a chaos of sacks, in which and in the midst of what seems a drifting snowstorm of letters and packets serried files of sorters are toiling.

We make a descent by the lift on its downward journey, and are on the floor of the Circulation Hall, in imminent danger, as it seems, of being overwhelmed by an avalanche compounded in equal proportion of sacks and porters. Somehow or other we struggle along a gangway between two tiers of sorting desks, till we find ourselves in a broader and clearer space that runs across the centre of the hall. At length there is a chance to use one's eyes without running the risk of being blinded by masses of the correspondence of London. The tables or sorting desks, covered with high-heaped masses of letters, extend to right and left of us in long rows, and at them stand thickly the busy sorters. On the opposite side of the sorting table is a row of sunken boxes, each representing a line of railway, with baskets above for the different London districts. There is something bewildering in the nimbleness with which letters fly into the boxes and baskets from the hands of the sorters; but nimble as the sorters are, we get an opportunity of a glimpse at the heaps of letters as they melt away before the rapid manipulation. Full of bright colors are these heaps to-night; they are studded all over with Christmas cards. Look at this golden-headed little one leaning over a partition, and contemplating with intensely bright, blue eyes, three extraordinarily gaudy-breasted robins pecking at crumbs, while the mild joke is printed on the wall of the mansion, "Poaching on a gentleman's preserves." On this other one behold disporting a bevy of tiny cupids and cupidesses rollicking in the merriment of blind man's buff. I am morally certain, too, that in those square envelopes, addressed in handwriting that is manifestly feigned, there are more Christmas cards. Paterfamilias, sitting in his glum City office, after he has signed the last check and written the last business letter, has engaged himself in laboriously feigning feminine caligraphy on this envelope, with intent to practice an innocent delusion on the young ones out at Clapham. Won't there be blank amazement to-morrow morning, when the postman brings the budget, as to who in the world could have sent the pretty cards; and won't mamma, who, of course, in the curtain conclave overnight has been intrusted with the profound secret, pretend to be the most amazed and bewildered of everybody, except papa himself, whose agony of speculation as to the identity of the sender will be something absolutely excruciating to behold! And there are other letters, too, that have a pleasant flavor of Christmas time about them, such as the one bearing the superscription, "From No. 420, Private John Smith, Forty-tenth Buffs, Bangalore, to Mrs. Smith, Beanstalk Village, by Chawfat, Broadhamptonshire. J. P. Swordknot, Colonel, commanding Forty-tenth Buffs." Honest Jack Smith, soldiering away out in India, has not forgotten the old mother that bore him, "though seas between them wide do roll," and he has dexterously timed his epistle so that the good dame will receive it as the village church-bells are chiming for the Christmas morning service.

Let us move down to the left where the packet tables are. Here the dispensation of Christmas presents by post falls heavily indeed on the toiling sorters. The piles of packets are nearly as high as their heads, impeding indeed their opportunity of a straight shoot at the boxes and baskets opposite to them. There are more than double the ordinary number of packets, and it is fair to reckon that the overplus are all Christmas presents. The packets are of all shapes and sizes. There are manifest toy books, addressed in great round hand, so that the specimens of the rising generation to whom they are addressed may be able to peruse the superscription, and so take care that no mistake occurs; boxes of games that rattle as you shake them; little bundles that emit mysterious squeaks when you squeeze them; packets of circular contour that may represent "the wonderful prismatic top" or the "Dancing Sailor, who dances most naturally on the self-winding color top (post free 12 stamps)." I could almost swear that this great packet — as to which I wonder how any letter-box could have taken it — contains a magic-lantern, and I tremble to think of the result if there should be oil in the lamp and it should escape into the miscellaneous correspondence. Here is a card with two dolls skewered upon it — one a big one the other a little one, and below the little one the pleading child-words, "I want to go home to Papa." There are Christmas cards here, too, at this packet table — whole handfuls of them — some comic, some sentimental; the comic preponderating over the sentimental. On some the addresses are on the reverse, and the sorters get impatient, and then laugh at their impatience as they look at the comical figures on the principal side; others carry their addresses written upon the shields borne by the desperately warlike and truculent-looking figures — invariably with long mustaches — which are delineated on them. There are piles of woollen material — comforters, cuffs; night-caps, I believe, although on this point I am not prepared to be positive; clouds of " clouds," as I am given to understand are styled those party-colored woollen streamers which ladies negligently intwine around their graceful forms, and wrought slippers innumerable. What profound mystery is hidden under this gorgeously-covered packet, athwart the top of which four Chinamen stalk, bearing on their shoulders the representation of a mighty chest, on the side of which is written an address with the instruction below, " Dear papa, please distribute?" Is that the seasonable present of a pair of skates, whose cover is so beshrouded with stamps as hardly to leave room for the address? It is unsatisfactory work to stand by the packet table guessing at the contents of packets, for the uncertainty ruins the romance. What you set down as a tiara of jewels may in reality be a set of false teeth, and the volume which you take to be an illustrated edition of the " History of Cockrobin," may be a treatise on conic sections or a work on veterinary surgery. But there is a spot where there need be no more unsatisfactory speculation, but where the secrets of a good many packets stand revealed. Just as in the buffets with this world of ours a good many of us get mauled and knocked about, so in their brief span of life, from the receiving-office to the sorting-table, not a few postal packets do not escape unscathed. The hurt ones are very tenderly dealt with. They are borne away to a side-table, which is called "the hospital"—and in this Post-office infirmary two clever surgeons dexterously stitch up their wounds, set all their broken limbs in splints, and in fine cure such of them as are at all curable, in a marvellously short space of time. Some of the patients seem past cure. Alas for the pretty box of bonbons that has burst open, and the contents of which are brought piecemeal into hospital, where the surgeon receives them with a shake of the head. *In extremis* seems this doll, whose integuments have been torn off, whose nose has been stove in, and one of whose nether limbs arrive some time after the frame to which it belongs. A bit of string tinkers up a box containing a lump of plum cake half cased in sugar, but there is no cure for this packet of Taddy's snuff, addressed in a woman's handwriting to a woman, and the contents whereof, pervading the atmosphere generally, set everybody a-sneezing. "The Devout Life" will live on with an extra slip of paper and a bit of sealing-wax. Decidedly "open for inspection" is the doll in this parcel; the head sticks up out of the paper, and something or other has given Madame a black eye. A pair of baby's shoes, with an inscription "from Auntie" pinned on them, have been sore battered as to cover, but the address is all right, and with luck baby will wear the pretty little boots, as she sits crowing on her mother's lap to-morrow night. A box of real roses, sent from France to Scarborough, has got broken, and some of the leaves fall on the surgeon's table as the delicious odor scents the air. With tender finger he handles the beautiful bouquet, and let us hope the fair one whose bosom it will adorn to-morrow night will scarcely be cognizant of the mishap. It makes one sorry to look on the damage that has be fallen this boxful of tiny dressed dolls, but the tender little things are gently repacked and fastened up. The trussed fowl in this package has not been seriously injured, nor has the snipe in this other, but the surgeon sniffs disgust at its high condition as he makes it fit for the road again. After all it is not so bad as the dead puppy which passed through his hands the other night. This morning he had to deal with a package of tallow candles, and a saveloy enveloped in tissue paper. As we gossip there is emptied out before him a curious medley. There is a smashed scent-bottle, whose contents have been mainly absorbed by a chignon addressed to a married lady. A woolly dog, that barks snappishly when he is handled, is half out of his paper kennel. A box of mistletoe has seriously suffered, but the doctor Gehülfe is dexterously to the front, and cherry lips may yet be kissed under it to-morrow night. Here are two ladies' caps, one — I love to be particular — in mauve with black beads, the other adorned with black flowers. Why didn't the gentleman who sent the beautiful bouquet to the lady in Surrey enclose it in a better box, and why, oh! why was not the dish of larks forwarded in something more substantial than a fragile case of paper, so as to avert the amalgamation into which they had entered with the contents of Master Jack's paint-box? "For dear Selina, with Aunt Anna's best love" is the inscription on a card that comes into hospital with what seems a miscellaneous heap of *débris*, but out of which the clever surgeons soon evolve order; and it is pleasant to see ultimately affixed to the envelopes of each their certificate of discharge, in the shape of a stamp bearing, that, having been found open, they have been refastened and forwarded.

But, alas! every thing that comes into hospital does not thus go out cured. No matter how skilled the medical men, there is no hospital but must have a deadhouse in its purlieus, and close by the St. Martin's-le-Grand Hospital for maimed letters, there is the deadhouse for such as have been posted with no address, or which have lost their addresses in the transit from the district post-offices. It must surely have been the tumultuous agitation of a throbbing heart which prevented the gentleman from affixing any address outside the neat case that enclosed the pretty emerald ear-rings, necklace, and cross, that he meant should have reached his lady-love on Christmas morning. The pocket-handkerchief with "Forget me not" daintily broidered on its corner, will scarcely reach its destination, lying there as it is in the deadhouse basket, not only without an address, but without a scrap of wrapper. What will Miss Cinderella do for lack of the twinkling little bottines that some one has posted to her, but off which the label has been torn? The poor child who sent the pencil-case with the paper round it on which is written in big text, "A present for papa," would weep bitter tears to-night if she knew her pretty present were lying in the deadhouse for want of an address; and it makes one's heart heavy to know that there will be no delivery to-morrow morning of the book-marker with "Forget me not" broidered on it, and round which, in great straggling letters, is the letter of the little one — "Darling Lily, wishing you a merry Christmas and a happy new year. You must please excuse the writing because it is so late." Lily's little sister has forgotten the address, perhaps "because it is so late;" and the card of Sister Ellen, of

Kensington, "To my sister, for thee my own sweet sister," has lost its envelope, if it ever had one. It may be submitted that a packet addressed to "Master C. Nisher," without another scrap of direction, is a scarcely sufficient address; and Master Nisher's Christmas present will, therefore, spend its Christmas in the deadhouse; as will, too, a beautiful pair of ear-rings in the form of tiny lapis lazuli shoes, girt with emerald rings, and most carefully packed; but posted unaddressed. From the hospital, it is but a step to the blind asylum, where two preternaturally acute gentlemen, with the help of directories, guides, and references of various kinds, are engaged in supplementing deficient addresses, and deciphering difficult ones. They are not easy to beat; but they cannot see their way to the transmission of a letter addressed to "Mr. J. Blomfield, Essex;" or of another from Germany, addressed "Herr J. Packendorff, Skene and Lydde."

While the bustle of the "Ordinary Correspondence" department is at its height, let us enter through the door in this partition, the smaller section of the hall in which the more complex system of the Registered Letter Department is conducted. Here every letter is verified by an elaborate series of checks, and a permanent record is taken of the address of every letter forwarded, while no letter is sent out without being tied up with green tape. Christmas affects this department quite as much as the other, for to-night there are over 6,000 registered letters, which is considerably more than a third above the average number. There is jewelry, you may be sure, in these neat little boxes, so carefully covered and sealed. On some tables there are piles of small square packets, each containing a watch. If you are not sure about the contents you may listen, and you will hear the watches ticking away industriously. Some watches are forwarded in another way — packed in little balls of hay or dry seaweed. There is no hospital here, for registered letters come from the district offices in a bag by themselves; but occasionally, nevertheless, there are mishaps. The superintendent once found a couple of clerks on the floor groping after quite a number of diamond rings, brooches, and ear-rings that had been shaken loose out of the bag on being emptied. It is odd to notice the little jewel boxes mingled with the portly letters of bankers, containing securities, shares, stock, or it may be bank-notes themselves. In the foreign registered department there is some extra pressure as elsewhere, it being calculated that about one-third of the whole number of letters are Christmas presents. But a large proportion of the foreign registered letters containing Christmas presents have gone already before to-night; with intent that they should duly complete their longer journey so as to reach their destination on Christmas morning. As soon as the registered letters are all dealt with, the bags — the registered letters go in green bags — are sealed up and taken out into the "ordinary correspondence" department, where they are inserted in the bags that are to hold the unregistered letters going to the same destinations.

But in this "ordinary correspondence" department, spite of the exertions made, the *ingens moles* of letters still broods over the scene, although it only wants a quarter to eight o'clock, and eight is the normal hour for clearing. To be clear by eight to-night is hopeless, but there is a special premium for celerity that every one seems determined to earn if possible. The heaps melt away as if by magic. What a German military writer calls the "order of disorder" reigns supreme. There is a frantic spasm as the clock strikes eight, and in a minute more one of the tables is clear. Others follow in quick succession. The letters already sorted into "divisions" and "railways" are whirled to the places where the "divisions" and "railways" are sorted into "roads," and then sorted into "towns." This operation is a very rapid one. The whole area of the hall is suddenly transformed into a billowy sea of sacks, which are rapidly stacked on trollies, and wheeled at the run through separate doors, out on to the loading-stage, which projects from the first-floor, on three sides of the Post-office. This platform is subdivided according to the different lines of railway carrying the mails. Above every shoot is a lettered lamp-light, below is a two-horse mail-cart. How the men in the mail-carts escape being embedded in the avalanche of mail-bags that descends upon them is a mystery. Ten minutes' intense exertion finishes the work as the clock chimes a quarter past eight. The folding lids of the carts are shut down, and the rattle of hoofs resounds on the stones, as "Royal Mail" after "Royal Mail" dashes off for the various stations. Close on sixty tons of letters, packets, and papers have been dealt with since six o'clock, and, bar accidents, all save those whose destination is very remote, will be delivered to-morrow morning. Among the mass go the Christmas presents of which we have written; all at least save the wretched ones in the deadhouse. Christmas Day is our British *jour de l'an*, and what has been written of a Christmas Eve in the Post-office will show that the kindly custom of Christmas presents prospers mightily. May the presents bring happiness and prosperity and a Merry Christmas, to the recipients, be they young or old, children or adults.

ON THE LINE OF MARCH.

AN AUTUMN MANŒUVRE SKETCH.

"Boots and saddles" have been followed by the "Turn out" and the "General parade;" the colonel has been round the ranks and given the word "Files right;" out to the front trots the Advance Guard, and the band follows close up. There are the three taps upon the kettledrums, and then at a signal from the bandmaster the musicians strike up a merry tune, and away goes the regiment on the line of march. The streets of Exeter, early as is the hour, are lined with spectators, kindly of face and pleasant of talk to the "horse-soldiers." The old pensioner at the street corner is the oracle of his group, and does not forget to recount to a listening audience how the "ould Thirteenth Light" rode in the first rank in the Light Cavalry charge at Balaclava. "See, there's the medal on the colonel's breast." The gay and gallant troopers get their heels down and their toes in, and with a sly touch of the bit and pressure of the leg set their horses a-capering just as that first-floor window is passed, which is full of pretty girls, who blush and giggle and pretend to turn away — but don't — as the passing horsemen kiss their hands, or by other gestures indicate susceptibility to their charms. The regiment has been in Exeter but a single night, yet it is surprising to any one who does not know the facility with which soldiers make friends what a number of acquaintances it owns already. Corporal Sabretasche bends low in the saddle to shake hands as he passes with the two sisters to whom last evening he did the honors of the camp. Trooper Swipes don't care so much about female acquaintances — there is hardly beer enough in their society for honest Bill; but he, too, has made some friends, and after he has shaken hands with the stout beer-house-keeper on the curbstone, he is observed to be stowing away in his haversack a soda-water bottle which you may depend does not contain soda-water. The town is cleared, and the regiment winds its way along a devious ascending lane in the open country. The word "ride at ease" passes from front to rear, and straightway pipes appear, and clouds of tobacco-smoke are wafted away over the hedgerows. Between scraps of barrack-room conversation, larded with barrack-room oaths, you hear comments on the beauty of the scenery and the pleasure of the travelling. Remember what "the line of march," with its variety, its jollity, its comparative freedom, is to these fellows, fresh from arid Aldershot, with its characteristics of sand, dirty singing-gaffs, the Long Valley, riding school, and "watering order" along the Farnborough road. The older soldiers have had nothing of this since the journey home from last year's Autumn Manœuvres; to the recruit it is a new world. He has heard so much in the barrack-room about the delights of the road; he pleaded so earnestly with his sergeant-major that he should be mounted, and not left behind; and now at last here he is, veritably "on the line of march." He put on his kit this morning as quickly as the sergeant-major's man himself; his horse he feels in rare fettle under him as the clever chestnut arches his neck, and steps proudly up the lane; he does not care who parades him — no, not if it were the Duke himself — and, in fine, he for the first time feels himself no more a barrack-square recruit, but a real, live, matured Hussar.

The hedgerows are all of a tangle with blossoming wild flowers, that trail their sprays into the narrow roadway, and flick the flies away from the ears of the troop horses. The balmy summer wind comes off the adjacent fields laden with the pleasant scent of the fresh hay, and rustles cheerfully among the tall standing wheat already begun to whiten into harvest. In front is a wood of dwarf oaks embedded in a floral undergrowth, out from which stick up great masses of gray rock, whose rugosities are softened by the tender leaves of the rock-ivy. Behind stretches wide one of the fairest prospects that this land of ours, rich beyond any other in fair prospects, can display. Below us, in a setting of emerald green, basks the smiling town of Exeter, its roofs, and streets, and gardens dominated by the fretwork towers of the Cathedral. The gentle green slopes beyond are partitioned into fields by hedgerows of darker green and flecked by clumps of trees. Here and there is a park, with its mansion-house embowered among ornamental timber, through which is fitfully visible the gleam of water. Below the town the valley becomes wider, and in the centre, far down, the broad bosom of the Exe shows itself between the frills of trees that fringe its margins. That white streak gleaming in the sunshine is Exmouth, and the still, glittering blue expanse beyond is the English Channel.

We have not lost this prospect, or ceased envying

the villagers of Longdown who abide continually in its fruition, when we overtake the regimental transport wagons, which, although they started earlier, have been retarded by the steepness of the hills. As the regiment passes them, they halt, and one notices that, although the transport is under the charge of a very efficient officer, the principal control of it is, at least in his own opinion, vested in "Billy," who superintends arrangements from the summit of one of the tarpaulins. "Billy" is the regimental dog. It is needless to say that he is hideously ugly, and that his cool assurance — in point of fact, his cheek — is on a par with his ugliness. I recommend to psychologists the study of the reason why there exists a mysterious affinity between soldiers and ugly dogs. A handsome dog turns up his nose at entering the troop-room, and when he looks in superciliously he is not invited to stay. But a bandy-legged, watery-eyed, kink-backed, stump-tailed wretch of a mongrel walks in with a hail-fellow-well-met manner, and forms up to the corporal for a bone in the frankest and homeliest spirit. Nor is he scouted. The uglier he is, the better he is liked. The men at first chaff him a little about his looks, just as they do an awkward recruit, but he outlives and rises superior to this good-humored contumely, and presently can afford to be himself patronizing. Once enlisted he is a soldier for life. He is not one of "Cardwell's men," who pledge themselves to the colors for a short term of service, and then are supposed — or rather were expected — to return to their native villages, and there foster morals and a love for soldiering. "Billy" has no native village, and it is to be feared no morals. He has thrown in his fate with the regiment, and when

the troop-ship sails which will by and by convey it to
India, Billy, squatting composedly on the topgallant
fok'sle or the long boat, will placidly contemplate the
fast receding shores of his native Britain, and later,
under the burning sun of an eastern clime, will no
doubt find all his energy called forth in the pursuit of
snapping at the calves of colored gentlemen. The
rear-guard are still enjoying the soft music of Billy's
yelp when the trumpet sounds "trot," and away
bumps the regiment jingling and clanking. The troop
horses, their breeding stirring in them, toss their heads
merrily, arch their crests to the bit, and carry themselves as proudly as if they were passing the Queen in
single file. Our recruit is in a rapture of exhilaration
by this time, and would not take his discharge if you
offered it to him without a penny of purchase-money
— almost a fabulous acme of a soldier's contentment
with his lot. A hill stops the trot by and by, and
hard by a water-mill on a pretty meadow the "halt"
is sounded, and the men swing themselves out of their
saddles, and stretch their legs and ease their horses.
Here, as at every cross-road, field-gate, and hamlet,
there is a little knot of country-folk gathered to see the
"soldiers" pass. Their geniality is dashed with a
certain respectful awe. They say "Sir" to the privates, touch their hats to the sergeants, and evidently
regard the colonel as quite on a par with the late Duke
of Wellington. The miller and his men, ay and his
frank-faced womenkind as well, bring out jugs and
pitchers of milk and pailfuls of fair cold spring-water,
and give unto the thirsty men to drink. And then
they convey by a respectful circumlocution their desire
to hear military music. They don't ask the colonel

that he bid the band strike up — that would, they seem to think, be too great a liberty ; but one " maid of the mill " says unto another, " Oh, shouldn't I just love to hear them instruments a-playing." And so " them instruments " do begin a-playing, and we move on with cheery adieux and good wishes from the population of the mill-hamlet. Then, down in the bottom, where the river, having passed in a broken rapid under a bridge, opens out into a broad deep pool girdled with alders, we come all of a sudden on the otter hounds owning merrily to a sprent. The dogs are speaking, splashing, and swimming to and fro, and the steep broken banks are being beaten by men with long sticks, while the field, consisting of half a dozen horsemen, whose enthusiasm is more sporting than their aspect, are either gathered in the road or have got through a gate into the meadow. Fain would the regiment linger to watch what sport ; but the march has to be completed, and the Queen's Regulations contain no provisions allowing incidental otter-hunting by the way. As the second " halt " sounds there slowly uprears himself from behind a heap of road gravel a bent, dilapidated man. He is old, he is round in the shoulders, he is set in the knees, on which are big knee-caps, for the man is a stone-breaker ; but the bent back and the bowed legs somehow straighten as the old fellow squares himself to his front, and brings up his hand to his forehead in a smart salute. Out of the saddle on to the stones, *facilis descensus* — and it is not alone troopers to whose lot the fate, often self-inflicted, falls. A man may have ridden in Pollock's rescue-column, and made the flinders fly in the hand-to-hand fighting at Chillianwallah, yet still come to a parish job at stone-breaking, while as yet the wrist, no longer supple for the sword-fence, can at least wield the chipping hammer. It does not do to question too closely. In the days when this old man soldiered there were pensions, and that he has not one and is at stone-breaking must be his own fault.

Away up the long narrow valley through the oak woods, with the little stream wimpling in the narrow streak of meadow below us. Why is it that when the word passes, "Singers to the front," and when each troop breaks into a rattling ringing chorus, the mellow strains of which fill the little valley with joy — why is it that good-looking Jack Bridoon singeth not, neither maketh merry with his fellows, but rides on abstractedly, with an occasional wistful look to the front? Honest Jack has been a fool like many a better man before him. On the march from Edinburgh to Aldershot Jack met a winsome Midland-county lass, and both being fain, nothing would please them but that they should get married. You wag your head sardonically, good madame, over "love in a cottage" when you are hinting to your fair daughter the detrimentality of Charlie Fraser, of the 115th Tigerslayers, who has his subaltern's pay and about £50 a year thrown in. It would astonish some people to know what is the private soldier's version of "love in a cottage" when he has married without leave, and has not his wife on the strength of the regiment. But Jack, if he had been selfish enough to marry when in the ranks, would not at least see his wife drabbing round the troop-rooms, scouring and shirt-washing for a wretched pittance. Jack's old folks live down Bridford way, and he sent the girl down to them, and turned teetotaller and gave up the pipe, that she might not be dependent on them for more than house-room. And some six months ago there came to Jack, as he lay in the Permanent Barracks, a letter in the crabbed pothooks of his old father, telling him that an event had occurred having a tendency to swell the population of Bridford. And so Jack is silent and pre-occupied to-day because he expects that by the finger-post at the top of the hill his winsome Midland-county girl will be waiting for him, with their boy in her arms for Jack's paternal inspection and approval. Well, what need one say anent a glimpse in passing of the flutter of a cotton dress, and of an eager loving face? Is it worth while to occupy space with the story of the unsensational little meeting, and of how his captain, with a kind word, tells Jack to fall out and come on with the baggage when it comes up two hours hence? No, let us ride on, and watch the pitching of the camp on breezy, high-lying Marden Down, from the top of which are visible the English Channel and the dim outline of the Welsh hills, on the further side of the Bristol Channel.

GEORGE MARTELL'S BUNDOBUST.[1]

GEORGE MARTELL was an indigo-planter in western Tirhoot, a fine tract of Bengal stretching from the Ganges to the Nepaul Terai, and roughly bounded on the west by the Gunduck, on the east by the Kussi. Planter-life in Tirhoot is very pleasant to a man in robust health, who possesses some resources within himself. In many respects it more resembles active rural life at home than does any other life led by Anglo-Indians. The joys of a planter's life have been enthusiastically sung by a planter-poet; and the frank genial hospitality of the planter's bungalow stands out pre-eminent even amidst the universal hospitality of India. The planter's bungalow is open to all-comers. The established formula for the arriving stranger is first to call for brandy-and-soda, then to order a bath, and finally to inquire the name of the occupant, his host. The laws of hospitality are as the laws of the Medes and Persians. Once in the famine-time a stranger in a palki reached a planter's bungalow in an outlying district, and sent in his card. The planter sent him out a drink, but did not bid him enter. The stranger remained in the veranda till sundown, had another drink, and then went on his way. This breach of statute-law became known. There was

[1] *Bundobust* is an Indian word, which, like many others, has been all but formally incorporated into Anglo-Indian English. Its meaning is plan, scheme, organized arrangement.

much excuse for the planter, for the traveller was a missionary, and in other respects was a *persona ingrata*. But the credit of planterhood was at stake; and so strong was the force of public opinion that the planter who had been a defaulter in hospitality had to abandon the profession, and quit the district. It was on this occasion laid down, as a guiding illustration, that if Judas Iscariot, when travelling around looking for an eligible tree on which to hang himself, had claimed the hospitality of a planter's bungalow, the dweller therein would have been bound to accord him that hospitality. Not even newspaper correspondents were to be sent empty away.

The indigo-planter is "up in the morning early," and away at a swinging canter on his "waler" nag, out into the *dahaut* to visit the *zillahs* on which his crop is growing. He returns when the sun is getting high with a famous appetite for a breakfast which is more than half luncheon. After his siesta, he may look in upon a neighbor — all Tirhoot are neighbors, and within a radius of thirty miles is considered next door. He would ride that distance any day to spend an hour or two in a house brightened by the presence of womanhood. His anxious period is *mahaye* time, when the indigo is in the vats, and the quantity and quality of the yield depend so much on care and skill. But except at *mahaye* time, he is always ready for relaxation, whether it takes the form of a polo-match, a pig-sticking expedition, or a race-meeting at Sonepoor, Muzzufferpore, or Chumparun. These race-meetings last for several days on end, there being racing and hunting on alternate days, with a ball every second night. It is worth a journey to India to see

Jimmy Macleod cram a cross-grained "waler" over an awkward fence, and squeeze the last ounce out of the brute in the run home on the flat. The Tirhoot ladies are in all respects charming; and it must remain a moot point with the discriminating observer whether they are more delightful in the genial home-circles of which they are the centres and ornaments, or in the more exciting stir and whirl of the ball-room. After every gathering, hecatombs of slain male victims mournfully cumber the ground; and one all-conquering fair one, now herself conquered by matrimony and motherhood, wrung ruefully from those her charms had blighted the title of "the destroying angel."

George Martell was an honest sort of a clod. He stood well with the ryots, and the mark of his factory always brought out keen bidding at Thomas's auction-mart in Mission-row, and was held in respect in the Commission Sale Rooms in Mincing-lane. He was a good shikaree, and could hold his own either at polo or at billiards; but being somewhat shy, and not a little clumsy, he did not frequent race-balls, nor throw himself in the way of "destroying angels." He had been over a dozen years in the district, and had not been known to propose once, so that he had come to be set down as something of a misogynist. Among his chief allies was a neighboring planter called Mactavish. Mactavish in some incomprehensible way — he being a gaunt, uncouth, bristly Scot, whose Highland accent was as strong as the whiskey with which he had colored his nose — had contrived to woo and win a bonny baby-faced girl, the ripple of whose laughter, and the dancing sheen of whose auburn curls, filled the Mactavish bungalow with glad bright sunshine. When Mac first brought home this winsome fairy, Martell had sheepishly shunned the residence of his friend, till one fine morning, when he came in from the *dahaut*, he found Minnie Mactavish quite at home among the pipes, empty sodawater bottles, and broken chairs that constituted the principal articles of furniture in his sitting-room. Minnie had come to fetch her husband's friend, and in her dainty imperious way would take no denial. So George had his bath, got a fresh horse saddled, nearly chucked Minnie over the other side as he clumsily helped her to mount her pony, and rode away with her a willing, if somewhat clownish, captive. Arriving at the bungalow Mactavish, honest George was bewildered by the transformation it had undergone. Flowers were where the spirit-case used to stand. There was a drawing-room with actually a piano in it; the *World* lay on the table instead of the *Sporting Times;* and the servants wore a quiet tasteful livery. Mac himself had been trimmed and titivated almost out of recognition. He who had been wont to lounge half the day in his pyjamahs was now almost smartly dressed; his beard was cropped, and his bristly poll brushed and oiled. If George had a weak spot in him, it was for a simple song well sung. Mrs. Mac, accompanying herself on the piano, sang to him "The Land o' the Leal," and brewed him a mild peg with her own fair hands. George by bedtime did not know whether he was on his head or his heels.

He lay awake all night thinking over all he had seen. Mactavish now was clearly a better man than ever he had been before. He had told George he was living more cheaply as a married man than ever he had done as a bachelor; and in the matter of happiness there was no comparison. George rose early to go home; but early as it was, Mrs. Mac was up too, and arrayed in a killing morning *negligé* that fairly made poor George stammer, gave him his *chota hazri*, and stroked his horse's nose as he mounted. About half-way home George suddenly shouted, "D—d if I don't do it too!" and brought his hand down on his thigh with a smack that set his horse buck-jumping.

In effect, George Martell had determined to get married. But where to find a Mrs. Martell? Mrs. Mactavish had told him she had no sisters, and that her only relative was a maiden grand-aunt, whom George thought must be a little too old to marry, unless in the last resort. If he took the field at the next race-meeting the fellows would chaff the life out of him; and besides, he scarcely felt himself man enough to face a "destroying angel." As he pondered, riding slowly homeward, a thought occurred to him. When he had been at home a dozen years ago, his two girl-sisters had been at school, and their great playmate had been a girl of eleven, by name Laura Davidson. Laura was a pretty child. He had taken occasional notice of her; had once kissed her, after having been severely scratched in the struggle; and had taken her and his sisters to the local theatre. What if Laura Davidson — now some three-and-twenty — were still single? What if she were pretty and nice? He remembered that the color of her hair was not unlike Mrs. Mac's, and was in ringlets too. And what if she were willing to come out and make lonely George Martell as happy a man as was that lucky old Mac?

It was mail-day, and George, taking time by the forelock, sat down and wrote to his sister what had come into his head. By the return mail he had her reply: Laura Davidson was single; she was nice; she was pretty; she had fair ringlets; she had a hazy memory of George and the kissing episode, and was willing to come out and marry him, and try to make him happy. But she could not well come alone; could George suggest any method of *chaperonage* on the voyage?

In the district of Chumparun, which in essentials is part of Tirhoot, lies the quaint little cavalry cantonment of Segowlie. It is the last relic of the old Nepaul war, which caused the erection of a chain of cantonments along the frontier, all of which, save Segowlie, are now abandoned. There is just room for one native cavalry regiment at Segowlie; and the soldiers like the station, because of excellent sport, and the good comradeship of the planters. At Segowlie, at the time I am writing of, there happened to be quartered a certain Major Freeze, whose wife, after a couple of years at home, was about returning to India. George had some acquaintance with the Major, and a far-off profound respect for his wife, who was an admirable and stately lady. It occurred to him to try whether it could not be managed that she should bring out the future Mrs. Martell. He saw the Major, who was only too delighted at the prospect of a new lady in the district, and the affair was soon arranged. Mrs. Freeze wrote that she and Miss Davidson were leaving by such-and-such a mail; and, knowing that Martell was rather lumpy when a lady was in the case, thoughtfully suggested that he should go down to Bombay and meet them; so as to get over the initial awkwardness by making himself useful, and gain his intended's respect by swearing at the niggers.

All went well. But George Martell was not quite his own master; he was only part of a "concern," and was bound to do his best for his partners. It happened, just about the time the P. & O. steamer was due at Bombay, that the most ticklish period of the indigo-planters' year was upon Martell. The juice had begun to flow from the vats. He had no assistant, and he did not dare to leave the work, so he telegraphed to Bombay to explain this to Mrs. Freeze, and added that he would meet her and her companion at Bankipore, where their long railway journey would end. Miss Davidson did not understand much about the absorbing crisis of indigo production, and she had a spice of romance in her composition; so that poor Martell did not rise in her estimation by his default at Bombay. When the ladies reached Bankipore there was still no Martell, but only a chuprassee with a note to say that the juice was still running, and he could not leave the factory, but would be waiting for them at Segowlie. At this even Mrs. Freeze almost lost her temper.

They have a "State Railway" now in Tirhoot, but at the time I am writing of there was only one *pukha* road in all the district. The ladies travelled in palanquins, or palkis, as they are more familiarly called. It is a long journey from Bankipore to Segowlie, and three nights were spent in travelling. Bluff old Minden Wilson stood on the bank above the ghât to welcome Mrs. Freeze across the Ganges. One day was spent at young Spudd's factory, the second at the residence of a genial planter rejoicing in the quaint name of Hong Kong Scribbens; on the third morning they reached Segowlie. But still no Martell; only a *chit* to say that that plaguy juice was still running, but he hoped to be able to drive over to dinner. Miss Davidson went to bed in a huff; and Major Freeze was temporarily inclined to think that her home-trip had impaired his good lady's amiability of character.

Martell did turn up at dinner-time. But he was hardly a man at any time to create much of an impression, and on this occasion he appeared to exceptional disadvantage. He was stutteringly nervous; and there were some evidences that he had been ineffectually striving to mitigate his nervousness by the consumption of his namesake. He had on a new dress-coat, which had not the remotest pretensions to fit him, and the bear's-grease which he had freely used gave unpleasant token of rancidity. The dinner was an unsatisfactory performance. Miss Davidson was extremely *distraite*, and Martell became more and more nervous as the meal progressed, and was manifestly relieved when the ladies retired. Soon after they had done so, the Major was sent for from the drawing-room. He found Miss Davidson sobbing on his wife's bosom. He asked what was the matter. The girl, with many sobbing interruptions, gasped out:

"He's the wrong man! O Heavens, I never saw *him* before! The man I remember who gave me sweets when I was a child had black hair; *he* has red! O, what shall I do? O, please send that man away, and let me go home!"

And then Miss Davidson went off into hysterics.

Here was a pretty state of matters! The Major and his wife could not see their way clear at all. Consultation followed consultation, with visits on the Major's part to poor Martell in the dining-room (irregularly interspersed). It was almost morning before affairs arranged themselves after a fashion. The new basis agreed upon was that the previously-existing arrangement should be regarded as dead, and that a courtship between Martell and Miss Davidson should be commenced *de novo* — he to do his best to recommend himself to the lady's affections, she to learn to love him if she could, red hair and all. And so George went home, and the Segowlie household went to bed.

Poor George at the best had a very poor idea of courting acceptably; and surely no man was more heavily handicapped in the enterprise prescribed him. He had to court to order, and to combat, besides, both the bad impression made at starting and the misfortune of his red hair. The poor fellow did his best. He used to come and sit in Mrs. Freeze's drawing-room hours on end, glowering at Miss Davidson in a silence broken by spasmodic efforts at forced talk. He brought the girl presents, gave her a horse, and begged of her to ride with him. But the great stupid fellow had not thought of a habit, and the girl felt a delicacy in telling him that she had not one. So the horse ate his head off in idleness, and George's heart went further and further down in the direction of his boots. He had so bothered Mrs. Freeze that she had washed her hands of him, and had bidden him worry it out on his own line.

In less than a month the crisis came. Miss Davidson could not bring herself to think of poor George as affording the makings of a husband. She told Mrs. Freeze so, and begged, for kindness' sake, that the Major would break this her determination to Mr. Martell, and desire him to give the thing up as hopeless. The Major thought the best course to pursue was to write to George to this effect. Next morning, in the small hours, the poor fellow turned up in the Segowlie veranda in a terribly bad way. He would not accept his fate at second-hand in this fashion; he must see Miss Davidson, and try to move her to be kind to him. In the end there was an interview between them, from which George emerged quiet, but very pale. His notable matrimonial bundobust had proved the deadest of failures; and the poor fellow's lip trembled as he thought of Mactavish's happy home and his own forlorn bungalow.

But although he had red hair, and did not know in the least what to do with his feet, George Martell was a gentleman. The lady continuing anxious to go home, he insisted on his right to pay her return passage as he had done her passage outward, urging rather ruefully that, he having taken a shot at happiness, and having missed fire, he must be the sole sufferer. It is a little surprising that this uncouth chivalry did not melt the lady; but she was obdurate; although she let him have his way about the passage money. So in the company of an officer's wife going home, Miss Davidson quitted Segowlie and journeyed to Bombay. Poor old George, with a very sore heart, was bent on seeing the last of her before settling down again to the old dull bachelor life. He dodged down to Bombay in the same train, travelling second class that he might not annoy the girl by a chance meeting; and stood with a sad face leaning on the rail of the Apollo Bunder, as he watched the ship containing his miscarried venture steam out of Bombay harbor on its voyage to England.

The same night he set out on his return to his plantation. At near midnight the mail-train from Bombay reaches Eginpoora, at the head of the famous Bhore ghât. Some refreshment is ordinarily procurable there, but it is not much of a place. George Martell had had a drink, and was sauntering moodily up and down the platform, waiting for the bell to ring. As he passed the second class compartment reserved for ladies, he heard a low tremulous voice exclaim, "O, if I could only make them understand that I'd give the world for a cup of tea!" George, if uncouth, was a practical man. His prompt voice rang out, "*Qui hye, ek pyala chah lao!* Promptly came the refreshment-room khitmutghar, hurrying with the tea; and George, taking off his hat, begged to know whether he could be of any further service.

It was a very pleasant face that looked out on him in the moonlight, and there was more than mere conventionality in the accents in which the pleasant voice acknowledged his opportune courtesy. Insensibly George and the lady drifted into conversation. She was very lonely, poor thing; a friendless girl coming out to be governess in the family of a *burra Sahib* at Chupra. Now Chupra is only across the Gunduck from Tirhoot, so George told his new acquaintance they were both going to nearly the same place, and professed his cordial willingness to assist her on the journey. He did so, escorting her right into Chupra before he set his face homeward; and he thenceforth got into a habit of visiting Chupra very frequently. Need I prolong the story? I happened to be in Bankipore when the Prince of Wales visited that focus of famine-wallahs. It fell to my pleasant lot to take Mrs. Martell in to dinner at the Commissioner's hospitable table. Mrs. Mactavish was sitting opposite; and I went back to my bedroom-tent in the compound without having made up my mind whether she or Mrs. Martell was the prettier and the nicer. So you see George Martell did not make quite so bad a *bundobust* after all.

REVERENCING THE GOLDEN FEET.

By Christmas, 1878, the winter had brought to a temporary standstill the operations of the British troops engaged in the first Afghan campaign, and I took the opportunity of this inaction to make a journey into Native Burmah, whose condition seemed thus early to portend the interest which almost immediately after converged upon it, because of King Thebau's wholesale slaughter of his relatives. Reaching Mandalay, the capital of Native Burmah, in the beginning of February, 1879, I immediately set about compassing an interview with the young king. Both Mr. Shaw, who was our resident at Mandalay at the time of my visit, and Dr. Clement Williams, whose kindly services I found so useful, are now dead; and many changes have occurred since the episode described below; but no description, so far as I am aware, has appeared of any visit to the Court of King Thebau of a later date than that made by myself some eighteen months ago.

One of my principal objects in visiting Mandalay, or, in Burmese phrase, of "coming to the Golden Feet," was to see the King of Burmah in his royal state, in the Presence Chamber of the Palace. Certain difficulties stood in the way of the accomplishment of this object. I had but a few days to spend in Mandalay. With the approval of Mr. Shaw, the British Resident, I determined to essay an informal course of action, and with this intent I enlisted the good offices of an English gentleman resident in Mandalay who has intimate relations with the Ministers and the Court.

This gentleman, Dr. Williams, was good enough to help me with zeal and address. The line of strategy to adopt was to interest in my cause one of the principal Ministers. Of these there are four, who constitute the Hlwot-dau, or High Court and Council of the Monarchy. These "Woonghys" or "Menghyis." as they are more commonly called — "Menghyi," meaning "Great Prince," — are of equal rank; but the senior Minister, the Yenangyoung Menghyi, who has precedence, was then in confinement, and, indeed, a decree of degradation had gone forth against him. Obviously he was of no use; but a more influential man than he ever was, and having the additional advantages of being at liberty, in power, and in favor, is the "Kingwoon Menghyi." He is in effect the Minister of the King of Burmah. His position is roughly equivalent to that of Bismarck in Germany, or of Gortschakoff in Russia, since in addition to his internal influence he has the chief direction of foreign affairs. Now this "Kingwoon Menghyi" had for a day or two been relaxing from the cares of State. Partly for his own pleasure, partly by way of example, he had laid out a beautiful garden on the low ground near the river. Within this garden he has the intention to build himself a suburban residence, which meanwhile is represented by a summer pavilion of teak and bamboo. He means that to the shady walks and pleasant rose groves of this garden the people of Mandalay shall have free access. He is a reformer, this "Kingwoon Menghyi," and believes in the humanizing effect of free access to the charms of nature. His garden laid out, and his pavilion finished, he was celebrating the event by a series of fêtes. He was " at home " in his pavilion to everybody; bands of music played all day long, and day after day in the kiosks among the young palm-trees and the rose bushes, Mandalay, high and low, made holiday in the mazy walks of his garden, and in an improvised theatre in a corner of it an interminable " poocy," or Burmese drama, was being enacted before ever varying and constantly appreciative audiences. Dr. Williams opined that it would conduce to the success of my object that we should call upon the Minister at his garden house and request him to use his good offices in my behalf.

It was near noon when we reached the entrance to the garden. Merry but orderly sight-seers thronged its alleys, and stared with wondering admiration at a rather attenuated jet of water which rose into the clear air some thirty feet above a rockwork fountain in the centre. Dignitaries strolled about under the stemless umbrellas, like huge shields, with which assiduous attendants protected them from the sun, and followed by a posse of retainers who prostrated themselves whenever their masters halted or looked round. Ladies in white jackets and trailing silk skirts of vivid hue, were taking a leisurely airing, each with her demure maid behind her, carrying the lacquer-ware box of betel nut. As often as not the fair ones were blowing copious clouds from huge reed-like cheroots. Sounds of shrill music were heard in the distance. Walking up the central alley between the rows of palms and the hedges of roses, we found in the veranda a mixed crowd of laymen and priests, the latter distinguishable by their shaved heads and yellow robes. The Minister was just finishing his morning's work of distributing offerings to the latter, in commemoration of the opening of his gardens. In response to a message, he at once sent to desire that we should come to him. The great "shoe-question," the *quæstio vexata* between British officialism and Burman officialism, did not trouble me. I had no official position; I wanted to gain an object. I have a respect for the honor of my country, but I cannot bring myself to realize that the national honor centres in my highlows. So I parted with them at the top of the steps leading up into the Minister's pavilion, and walking on what is known as my "stocking feet," and feeling rather shuffling and shabby accordingly, was ushered through a throng of prostrate dependants into the presence of the Menghyi. He came forward frankly and cordially, shook hands with a hearty smile with myself and Dr. Williams, and beckoned us into an inner alcove, carpeted with rich rugs, and panelled with mirrors. Placing himself in a half-sitting, half-kneeling attitude, which did not expose his feet, he beckoned to us to get down also. I own to extreme difficulty in keeping my feet out of sight, which is a point *de rigueur;* but his Excellency was not censorious. There was with him a secretary, who had resided several years in Europe, and who spoke fluently English, French, and Italian. This gentleman knew London thoroughly, and was perfectly familiar both with the name of the *Daily News* and of myself. He introduced me formally to his Excellency, who, I ought to have mentioned, was the head of the Burmese Embassy which visited Europe a few years ago. That his Excellency had some sort of knowledge of the *Daily News* was obvious from the circumstance that when its name was mentioned he nodded and exclaimed, "Ah! Ah! Gladstone, Bright!" in tones of manifest approval, which may be accounted for by the fact that he himself is a pronounced Liberal. I explained that I had come to Mandalay to learn as much about Burmese manners, customs, and institutions as was possible in four days, with intent to embody my impressions in letters to England, and that as the king was the chief institution of the country, I had a keen anxiety to see him, and begged of his Excellency to lend me his aid toward doing so. He gave no direct reply, but certainly did not frown on the request. We were served with tea (without cream or sugar) in pretty china cups, and then the Menghyi, observing that we were looking at some quaint-shaped musical instruments at the foot of the dais, explained that they belonged to a band of rural performers from the Pegu district, and proposed that we should first hear them play, and afterwards visit the theatre and witness the "pooey." We assenting, he led the way from his pavilion through the garden to a pretty kiosk, half embosomed in foliage, and chairs having been brought the party sat down. We had put on our shoes as we quitted the dais. The Menghyi explained that it was pleasanter for him, as it must be for us, that he should change the manner of our reception from the Burmese to the European custom; and we were quite free to confess that we would sooner sit in chairs than squat on the floor. More tea was brought, and a plateful of cheroots. After we had sat a little while in the kiosk, we were joined by the chief Under Secretary for Foreign Affairs, the Baron de Giers of Burmah, a jovial, corpulent elderly gentleman, who had the most wonderful likeness to the late Pio Nono, and who clasped his brown hands over his fat paunch, and kicked about his plump, bare brown feet in high enjoyment when any thing that struck him as humorous was uttered. He differed in appearance *toto cœlo* from his superior, who was a lean-faced and lean-figured man, grave and indeed somewhat sad both of eye and of visage when his face was in repose. As we talked, our conversation being through the interpreting secretary, there came to the curtained entrance to the kiosk a very dainty little lady. I had noticed her previously sauntering around the garden under one of the great shield-like shades, with a following of serving men and serving women behind her. She greeted the Menghyi very prettily, with the most perfect composure, although strangers were present. She was clearly a great pet with him: he took her on his knee and played with her long black hair, as he told her about the visitors. The little miss was in her twelfth year, and was the daughter of a colleague and a relative of the Menghyi. She had an olive oval face, with lovely dark eyes, like the eyes of a deer. She wore a tiara of feathery white blossoms. In her ears were rosettes of chased red gold. Round her throat was a necklace of a double row of large pearls. Her fingers — I regret to say they were not very clean — were loaded with rings set with great diamonds of exceptional sparkle and water; one stone in particular must have been worth many thousands of pounds. She wore a jacket of white silk, and round her loins was girt a gay silken robe that trailed about her bare feet as she walked. She shook hands with us with a pretty shyness, and immediately helped herself to a cheroot, affably accepting a light from mine. The Menghyi told us she was a great scholar — could read and write with facility, and had accomplishments to boot.

By this time the provincial band had taken its place under one of the windows of the kiosk, and it presently struck up. Its music was not pretty. There were in the strange weird strain suggestions of gongs, bagpipes, penny whistles, and the humble tom-tom of Bengal. The gentleman who performed on an instrument that seemed a hybrid between a flute and a French horn occasionally arrested his instrumental to favor us with vocal strains, but he failed to compete successfully with the cymbals. I do not think the Menghyi was enraptured by the music of the strollers from Pegu, for he presently asked us whether we were ready to go to the "pooey." He again led the way through the garden, passing in one corner of it a temporary house, of which a company of Burmese nuns, short-haired, pallid-faced, unhappy-looking women, were in possession, and passing through a gate in the wicker-work fence ushered us into the "state-box" of the impoverished theatre. There is very little labor required to construct a theatre in Burmah. Over a framework of bamboo poles stretch a number of squares of matting as a protection from the sun. Lay some more down in the centre as a flooring for the performers. Tie a few branches round the central bamboo to represent a forest, the perpetual set-scene of a Burmese drama, and the house is ready. The performers act and dance in the central square laid with matting. A little space on one side is reserved as a dressing and green-room for the actresses; a similar space on the other side serves the turn of the actors; and then come the spectators crowding in on all four sides of the square. It is an orderly and easily-managed audience; it may be added an easily-amused audience. The youngsters are put — or put themselves — in the front, and squat down; the grown people kneel or stand behind. Our "state-box" was merely a raised platform laid with carpets and cushions, from which as we sat we looked over the heads of the throng squatting under and in front of us. Of the drama I cannot say that I carried away with me particularly clear impressions. True, I only saw a part of it — it was to last till the following morning; but long before I left the plot to me had become bewilderingly involved. The opening was a ballet; of that at least I am certain. There were six lady dancers, and six gentlemen ditto. The ladies were arrayed in splendor, with tinsel tiaras, necklaces, and bracelets, gauzy jackets, and waving scarfs; and long, light, clinging silken robes, of which there was at least a foot on the "boards" about their feet. They were old, they were ugly, they leered fiendishly; their faces were plastered with powder in a ghastly fashion, and their coquetry behind their fans was the acme of caricature. But my pen halts when I would describe the gentlemen dancers. I believe that in reality they were not meant to represent fallen humanity at all; but were intended to personify "nats," the spirits or princes of the air of Burmese mythology. They carried on their heads pagodas of tinsel and colored glass that towered imposingly aloft. They were arrayed in tight-bodiced coats with aprons before and behind of fantastic outline, resembling the wings of dragons and griffins, and these coats were an incrusted mass of spangles and pieces of colored glass. Underneath a skirt of tartan silk was fitfully visible. Their brown legs and feet were bare. The expression of their faces was solemn, not to say lugubrious — one performer had a most whimsical resemblance to Mr. Toole when he is sunk in an abyss of dramatic woe. They realized the responsibilities of their position, and there were moments when these seemed too many for them. The orchestra, taken as a whole, was rather noisy; but it comprised one instrument, the "bamboo-harmonicon," which deserves to be known out of Burmah because of its sweetness and range of tone. There were lots of "go" in the music, and every now and then one detected a kind of echo of a tune not unfamiliar in other climes. One's ear seemed to assure one that *Madame Angot* had been laid under contribution to tickle the ears of a Mandalay audience, yet how could this be? The explanation was that the instrumentalists, occasionally visiting Thayet-myo, or Rangoon, listen there to the strains of our military bands, and adapt these to the Burmese orchestra in some deft, inscrutable manner, written music being unknown in the musical world of Burmah.

Next day the Kingwoon Menghyi took the wholly unprecedented step of inviting to dinner the British Resident, his suite, and his visitor — myself. Mr. Shaw accepted the invitation, and I considered myself specially fortunate in being a participator in a species of intercourse at once so novel, and, to all seeming, so auspicious.

About sundown the Residency party, joined *en route* by Dr. Williams, rode down to the entrance to the gardens. Here we were warmly received by the English-speaking Secretary, and by the jovial bow-windowed Minister who so much resembles the late Pio Nono. We were escorted to the veranda of the pavilion, where the Menghyi himself stood waiting to greet us, and were ushered up to the broad, raised, carpeted platform, which may be styled the drawing-room. Here was a semi-circle of chairs. On our way to these, a long row of squatting Burmans was passed. As the Resident approached, the Menghyi gave the word, and these stood erect in a line. He explained that they were the superior officers of the army quartered in the capital — generals, he called them — whom he had asked to meet us. Of these officers one commanded the eastern guard of the Palace, the other the western; two others were aides-de-camp after a fashion. Just as the Menghyi and his subordinate colleagues represented the Ministry, so these military people represented the Court. The former was the moderate constitutional element of the gathering; the latter the "jingo" or personal government element, for the Burmese Court is re-actionary, and these military sprigs are of the personal suite of the King, and are understood to abet him in his falling away from the constitutional promise with which his reign began. Their presence rendered the occasion all the more significant. That they were deputed from the palace to attend and watch events was pretty certain, and indeed the two aides went away immediately after dinner, their excuse being that his Majesty was expecting their personal attendance. After a little while of waiting, the *mauvais quart d'heure* having the edge of its awkwardness taken off by a series of introductions, dinner was announced, and the Menghyi, followed by the Resident, led the way into the adjoining *salle à manger*. Good old Pio Nono, who, I ought to have said, had been with the Menghyi, a member of the Burmese embassy to Europe, jauntily offered me his arm, and gave me to understand that he did so in compliance with English fashion. The Resident sat on the right of the Menghyi, I was on his left; the rest of the party, to the number of about fifteen, took their places indiscriminately. Mr. Andrino, an Italian in Burmese employ, being at the head of the table, Dr. Williams at the foot. Our meal was a perfectly English dinner, served and eaten in the English fashion. The Burmans had taken lessons in the nice conduct of a knife and fork, and fed themselves in the most irreproachably conventional manner, carefully avoiding the use of a knife with their fish. Pio Nono, who sat opposite the Menghyi, tucked his napkin over his ample paunch and went in with a will. He was in a most hilarious mood, and taxed his memory for reminiscences of his visit to England. These were not expressed with useless expenditure of verbiage, nor did they flow in unbroken sequence. It was as if he dug in his memory with a spade, and found every now and then a nugget in the shape of a name, which he brandished aloft in triumph. He kept up an intermittent and disconnected fire all through the dinner, with an interval between each discharge. "White-bait!" "Lord Mayor!" "Fishmongers!" "Cremorne!" "Crystal Palace!" "Edinburgh!" "Dunrobin!" "Newcastle!" "Windsor!" each name followed by a chuckle and a succession of nods. The Menghyi divided his talk between the Resident and myself. He told me that of all the men he had met in England his favorite was the Duke of Sutherland; adding that the duke was a nobleman of great and striking eloquence, a trait which I had not been in the habit of regarding as markedly characteristic of his grace. He spoke with much warmth of a pleasant visit he had paid to Dunrobin, and said he should be heartily glad if the duke would come to Burmah, and give him an opportunity of returning the hospitality. Here Pio Nono broke in with one of his periodical exclamations. This time it was "Lady Dudley." Of her and of her husband the Menghyi then recalled his recollections, and if more courtly tributes have been paid to her ladyship's charms and grace, I question if any have been heartier and more enthusiastic than the appreciation of this Burmese dignitary. The soldiers were somewhat stiff, but as the dinner proceeded the generals warmed in conversation with the Resident. But the aides were obstinately supercilious, and only partially thawed in acknowledgment of compliments on the splendor of their jewelry. Functionaries attached to the personal suite of his Majesty wear huge ear-gems as a distinguishing mark. The aides had these in blazing diamonds, and were good enough to take out the ornaments and hand them round. The civil ministers wore no ornaments, and their dress was studiously plain. We were during dinner entertained by music, instrumental and vocal, sedulously modulated to prevent conversation from being drowned. The meal lasted quite two hours, and when it was finished the Menghyi led the way to coffee in one of the kiosks of the garden. I should have said that no wine was on the table at dinner. The Burmans by religion are total abstainers, and their guests were willing to follow their example for the time and to fall in with their prejudices.

After coffee we returned to the drawing-room, and listened to a concert. The only solo-vocalist was the prima donna par excellence, Mdlle. Yeendun Malé. The burden of her songs was love, but I could not succeed in having the specific terms translated. Then she sang an ode in praise of the Resident, and gracefully accepted his pecuniary appreciation of her performance. Pio Nono then beckoned to her to flatter me at close quarters, but, mistaking the index, she addressed herself to the Residency chaplain, in strains of hyperbolical encomium. The mistake having been set right, much to the reverend gentleman's relief, the songstress overpowered my sensitive modesty by impassioned requests in verse that I should delay my departure; that, if I could not do that, I would take her away with me; and that, if this were beyond my power, I should at least remember her when I was far away. The which was an allegory, and cost me twenty rupees.

When the good-nights were being said, the Menghyi gratified me by the information that the King had given his consent to my presentation, and that I was to have the opportunity, next morning, of "reverencing the Golden Feet."

The Royal Palace occupies the central space of the city of Mandalay. It is almost entirely of woodwork, and is not only the counterpart of the palace which Major Phayre saw at Amarapoora, but the identical palace itself, conveyed piecemeal from its previous site, and re-erected here. Its outermost enclosure consists of a massive teak palisading, beyond which all round is a wide clear space laid out as an esplanade, the further margin of which is edged by the houses of ministers and court officials. The Palace enclosure is a perfect square, each face about three hundred and seventy yards. The main entrance, the only one in general use, is in the centre of the Eastern face, almost opposite to which, across the esplanade, is the Yoom-dau, or High Court. This gate is called the "Yive-dau-yoo-Taga," or the "Royal Gate of the Chosen," because the charge of it is intrusted to chosen troops. As I passed through it on my way to be presented to his Majesty, the aspect of the "chosen" troops was not imposing. They wore no uniform, and differed in no perceptible item from the common coolies of the outside streets. They were lying about on charpoys and on the ground, chewing betel or smoking cheroots, and there was not even the pretence of sentries under arms. Some rows of old flint-lock guns stood in racks in the gateway, rusty, dusty, and untended; they might have been untouched since the last insurrection. Crossing an intermediate space overgrown with shrubbery, we passed through a high gateway cut in the inner brick wall of the enclosure; and there confronted us the great Myenan of Mandalay—the Palace of the "Sun-descended Monarch." The first impression was disappointing, for the whole front was covered with gold-leaf and tawdry tinsel-work, which had become weather-worn and dingy. But there was no time now to halt, inspect details, and rectify perchance first impressions. A message came that the Kingwoon Menghyi, my host of the previous evening — substantially the Prime Minister of Burmah — desired that we, that is Dr. Williams, my guide, philosopher, and friend, and myself, should wait upon him in the Hlwot-daù, or Hall of the Supreme Council, before entering the Palace itself. The Hlwot-daù is a detached structure on the right front of the Palace as one enters by the Eastern gate. It is the Downing Street of Mandalay. Its sides are quite open, and its fantastic roof of grotesquely carved teak, plastered with gilding, painting, and tinsel, is supported on massive teak pillars, painted a deep red. Taking off our shoes, we ascended to the platform of the Hlwot-daù, where we found the Menghyi surrounded by a crowd of minor officials and suitors, squatting on their stomachs and elbows, with their legs under them and their hands clasped in front of their bent heads. The Menghyi came forward several paces to meet us, conducted us to his mat, and sitting down himself, and bidding us do the same, explained that, as it was with him a busy day, he would not be able personally to present me to the King, as he had hoped to have done, but that he had made all the arrangements, and had delegated the charge of us to our old friend whom I have ventured to call "Pio Nono." That corpulent and jovial worthy made his appearance at this moment, along with his English-speaking subordinate, and with cordial acknowledgments and farewells to the Menghyi we left the Hlwot-daù under their guidance. They led us along the front of the Palace, passing the huge gilded cannon that flanked either side the central steps leading up into the throne room, and turning round the northern angle of the Palace front, conducted us to the Hall of the Bya-dyt, or Household Council. We had to leave our shoes at the foot of the steps leading up to it. The Bya-dyt is a mere open shed, its lofty roof borne up by massive teak timber. What splendor has been its, in the matter of gilding and tinsel, has greatly faded. The gold-leaf has been worn off the pillars by constant friction, and the place appears to be used as a lumber-room, as well as a council chamber. On the front of one of a pile of empty cases was visible, in big black letters, the legend " Peek, Frean, and Co., London." State documents reposed in the receptacle once occupied by biscuits. Clerks lay all around on the rough dusty boards, writing with agate styles on tablets of black papier-maché ; and there was a constant flux and reflux of people of all sorts, who appeared to have nothing to do, and who were doing it with a sedulously lounging deliberation that seemed to imply a gratifying absence of arrears of official work. We sat down here for a while along with Pio Nino and his assistant, who busied himself in dictating to a secretary a description of myself and a catalogue of my presents to be read by the herald to his Majesty when I should be presented. Then Pio Nino went away and presently came back saying that it was intended to bestow upon me some souvenirs of Mandalay, and to admit of the preparation of these the audience would not take place for an hour or so. He invited us in the mean time to inspect the public apartments of the Palace itself and the objects of interest within the Palace enclosure. So we got up, and still without our shoes, walked through the suite leading to the principal throne room or great hall of audience.

These are simply a series of minor throne rooms. The first one in order from the private apartments is close to the Bya-dyt. Pray bear in mind that the whole suite, including the great audience hall, are not rooms at all in our sense of the word. They are simply open-roofed spaces, the roofs gabled, spiked, and carved into fantastic shapes, laden with dingy gold-leaf, garishly picked out with glaring colors, and studded with bits of stained glass, the roofs, or rather, I should say, the one continuous roof, supported on massive deep red pillars of teak wood. The whole Palace is raised from the ground on a brick platform, some ten feet high. The partitions between the several halls are simply skirtings of planking covered with gold-leaf. The whole Palace seems an armory. Some ten or twelve thousand stand of obsolete muskets are ranged along these partitions and crammed into the ante-room of the throne-room proper. The whole suite is dingy, dirty, and uncared for; but on a great day, with the gilding renewed, carpets spread on the rugged boards, banners waving, and the courtiers in full dress, no doubt the effect is materially improved. The vista from the throne of the great hall of audience looks right through the columned arcade to the "Gate of the Chosen," and that we might imagine the scene more vividly we considered ourselves as on our way to Court on one of the great days, and going to the gate again began anew. The pillared front of the Palace stretched before us, raised on the terrace, its total length 260 feet. Looking between the two gilded cannon we saw at the foot of the central steps a low gate of carved and gilded wood. That gate is never opened except to the King — none save he may use these central steps. Raising our eyes we look right up the vista of the hall to the lofty throne raised against the gilded partition that closes at once the vista and the hall. We have been looking down the great central nave, as it were, toward the west gate, in the place of which is the throne. But along the eastern front of the terrace runs a long colonnade, whose wings form transepts at right angles to the nave. The throne-room is shaped like the letter T, the throne being at the base of the letter, and the cross-bar representing the colonnade. Entering at the extremity of one of these, we traverse it to the centre, and then face the nave. The throne is exactly before us, at the end of the pillared vista. Five steps ascend to its dais. Its form is peculiar, contracting by a gradation of steps from the base upwards to mid-height, and again expanding to the top, which is a cushioned ledge such as is seen in the box of a theatre. On the platform, which now is bare planks, the King and Queen, on a great reception day, sit on gorgeous carpets. The entrance is through gilded doors from a staircase in the ante-room beyond. There is a rack of muskets round the foot of the throne, and just outside the rails a half-naked soldier lay snoring. Our Burman companion assured us that, seeing it now in its condition of dismantled tawdriness, I could form no idea of the fine effect when King and Court in all their splendor were gathered in it on a ceremonial day. I tried to accept his assurances, but it was not easy to imagine such forlorn dinginess changed into dazzling splendor. Just over the throne, and in the centre of the palace and of the city, rises in gracefully diminishing stages of fantastic wood-carving, a tapering *phya-sath* or spire, similar to those surmounting sacred buildings, and crowned with the gilded *Htee*, an honor which royalty alone shares with ecclesiastical sanctity. The spire, like every thing else, has been gilt, but it is sadly tarnished, and has lost much of its brilliancy of effect.

Having looked at the Hall of Audience, we strolled through the Palace esplanade. A wall parts off this from the private apartments and the pleasure-grounds, occupying the western section of the Palace enclosure. A series of carved and gilded gables, roofed with glittering zinc plates, is visible over the wall. The grounds are said to be well planted with flowering shrubs and fruit trees, and contain lakelets and rockeries. Built against the outer wall, and facing the enclosed space, are barracks for soldiers, and gun sheds. The accommodation is as primitive as are the weapons, and that is saying a good deal. Pio Nono led us across to a big wooden house, scarcely at all ornamented, which is the every day abode of the "Lord White Elephant." His "Palace" or State apartment was not pointed out to us. His lordship, in so far as his literal claim to be styled a white elephant, is an impostor of the deepest dye, and a very grim and ugly impostor to boot. He is a great, lean, brown, flat-sided brute, his ears, forehead, and trunk mottled with a dingy cream color. But he belongs, all the same, to the lordly race. "White elephants" are a science, which has a literature of its own. According to this science, it is not the whiteness that is the criterion of a white elephant. So much, indeed, the reverse, that a "white elephant," according to the science, may be a brown elephant in actual color. The points are the mottling of the face, the shape and color of the eyes, the position of the eyes, and the length of the tail. It is certain that the "lord white elephant" has, to the most cursory observation, a peculiar and abnormal eye. The iris is yellow, with a reddish outer annulus, and a small, clear, black pupil. It is essentially a shifty, treacherous eye, and I noticed that everybody took particularly good care to keep out of range of his lordship's trunk and tusks. The latter are superb, long, massive, and smooth, their tips quite meeting far in front of his trunk. His tail is much longer than in the Indian elephants, and is tipped with a bunch of long, straight black hair. Altogether he is an unwholesome, disagreeable-looking brute, who munches his grass morosely, and has no elephantine geniality. He is a youngster — the great, old, really white elephant which Yule describes died some time ago, after an incumbency dating from 1806. The "White Elephant" is never ridden now, but the last King but one used frequently to ride his predecessor, acting as his own mahout. We did not see his trappings, as our visit was paid unawares, when he was quite in undress; but Yule says that when arrayed in all his splendor his headstall is of fine red cloth, studded with great rubies, interspersed with valuable diamonds. When caparisoned he wears on his forehead, like other Burmese dignitaries, including the King himself, a golden plate inscribed, with his titles, and a gold crescent set with circles of large gems between the eyes. Large silver tassels hang in front of his ears, and he is harnessed with bands of gold and crimson and gold, set with large bosses of pure gold. He is a regular "estate of the realm," having a woon or minister of his own, four gold umbrellas, the white umbrellas which are peculiar to royalty, with a large suite of attendants, and an appanage to furnish him with maintenance wherewithal. When in state his attendants leave their shoes behind them when they enter the Palace. In a shed adjacent to that occupied by the "Lord White Elephant" stands his lady wife, a browner, plumper, and generally more amiable-looking animal. Contrary to universal experience elsewhere, elephants in Burmah breed in captivity, but this union is unfertile, and the race of "Lord White Elephants" must be maintained *ab extra*. The so-called white elephants are sports of nature, and of no special breed. They are called Albinoes, and are more plentiful in the Siam region than in Burmah.

By this time the hour was approaching that had been fixed for the presentation, and we returned to the Bya-dyt. The summons came almost immediately. Ushered by Pio Nono, and accompanied by several courtiers, we traversed some open passages, and finally reached a kind of pagoda or kiosk within the private gardens of the Palace. The King was not to appear in state, and this place had been selected by reason of its absolute informality. There was no ornament anywhere. Not so much as a speck of gilding or an atom of tinsel. We reached and squatted down on a low platform covered with grass matting, through which pierced the teak columns supporting the lofty roof. A space had been reserved for us in the centre, on either side of which, their front describing a semi-circle, a number of courtiers lay crouching on their stomachs, but placidly puffing cheroots. On our left were two or three superior military officers of the Palace Guard, distinguishable only by their diamond ear-jewels. My presents — they were trivial: an opera-glass, a few boxes of chocolate, and a work-box — were placed before me as I sat down. There were other offerings to right and to left of them — a huge bunch of cabbages, a basket of Kohl-rabi, and three baskets of orchids. In the clear space in front I observed also a satin robe lined with fur, a couple of silver boxes, and a ruby ring. These, I imagined, were also for presentation, but it presently appeared they were his Majesty's return gifts for myself. Before us, at a higher elevation, there was a plain wooden railing with a gap in the centre, and the railing enclosed a sort of recess that looked like a garden-house. Over a ledge where the gap was, had been thrown a rich crimson and gold trapping, that hung low in front, and on the ledge were a crimson cushion, a betel box, and a tall oval spittoon in gold set with pearls. A few minutes passed, beguiled by conversation in a low tone, when six guards, armed with double-barrelled fire-arms of very diverse patterns, mounted the platform from the left side, and took their places on either side, squatting down. The guards wore black silk jackets lined with fur, and scarlet kerchiefs bound round their heads. Then a door opened in the left side of the garden-house, and there entered first an old gaunt beardless man — the chief eunuch — closely followed by the King, otherwise unattended. He came on with a quick step, and sat down, resting his right arm on the crimson cushion on the ledge in the centre of the railing. He wore a white silk jacket, and *loonghi*, or petticoat robe, of rich yellow and green silk. His only ornaments were his diamond ear-jewels. As he entered all bent low, and when he had seated himself, a herald lying on his stomach read aloud my credentials. The literal translation is as follows: " So-and-so, a great newspaper teacher of the *Daily News* of London, tenders to his Most Glorious Excellent Majesty, Lord of the Ishaddan, King of Elephants, master of many white elephants, lord of the mines of gold, silver, rubies, amber, and the noble serpentine, Sovereign of the Empires of Thunaparanta and Tampadipa, and other great empires and countries, and of all the umbrella-wearing chiefs, the supporter of religion, the Sun-descended Monarch, arbiter of life, and great, righteous King, King of Kings, and possessor of boundless dominions and supreme wisdom, the following presents." The reading was intoned in a comical high recitative, strongly resembling that used when our Church service is intoned; and the long-drawn " Phya-a-a-a-a " (my lord) which concluded it, added to the resemblance, as it came in exactly like the " Amen " of the Liturgy.

The reading over, the return presents were picked up by an official, and bundled over to me without any ceremony, the King meanwhile looking on in silence, chewing betel and smoking a cheroot. Several of the courtiers were following his example in the latter respect. Presently the King spoke in a distinct deliberate voice.

" Who is he? "

Dr. Williams, acting as my introducer, replied in Burmese, —

" A writer of the *Daily News* of London, your Majesty."

" Why does he come? "

" To see your Majesty's country, and in the hope of being permitted to reverence the Golden Feet."

"Whence does he come?"

"From the British army in Afghanistan, engaged in war against the Prince of Cabul."

"And does the war prosper for my friends the English?"

"He reports that it has done so greatly, and that the Prince of Cabul is a fugitive."

"Where does Cabul lie in relation to Kashmir?"

"Between Kashmir and Persia, in a very mountainous and cold region."

There had been pauses more or less long between each of these questions; the King obviously reflecting what he should ask next, then there was a longer, and, indeed, a wearisome pause. Then the King spoke again.

"Where is the Kingwoon Menghyi?"

"In Court, your Majesty," replied Pio Nono. "It is a Court day."

"It is well. I wish the Ministers to make every day a Court day, and to labor hard to give prompt justice to suitors, so that there be no complaint of arrears."

With this laudable injunction, his Majesty rose and walked away, and the audience was over.

The King of Burmah, when I saw him, was little over twenty, and he had been barely four months on the throne. He was a tall, well-built, personable young man, very fair in complexion, with a good forehead, clear, steady eyes, and a firm but pleasant mouth. His chin was full, and somewhat sensual-looking, but withal he was a manly, frank-faced young fellow, and was said to have gained self-possession, and lost the early nervous awkwardness of his new position with great rapidity. Circumstances had even then occurred to prove that he was very far from destitute of a will of his own, and that he had no fondness for any diminution of the Royal Prerogative. As we passed out of the Palace after the interview, a house in the Palace grounds was pointed out to me within which had been imprisoned in squalid misery, ever since the mortal illness of the late King, a number of the members of the Burmese blood-royal.

P.S.—A few days after my visit, all these were massacred with fiendish refinements of cruelty.

CHRISTMAS DAY ON A "GROWLER."

It was not quite an easy thing to carry into effect the idea which occurred to me, that it would be a novel and perhaps interesting experience to spend Christmas Day in the capacity of the driver of a four-wheel cab. "Cauliflower Bill" was as hard to be persuaded as any stiff-necked Israelite of old. "Cauliflower Bill" — so nicknamed, as I learned, from the marked prominence and number of grog blossoms on his nose, which he found it necessary to powder profusely to mitigate the danger of erysipelas or some such disorder — "Cauliflower Bill" was the owner of a single cab and of a pair of horses, and I had made overtures to him, having been acquainted with him for some time, under the belief that he would be a likely man to serve my turn, as he would not run so much risk in lending me his badge for the day as would a man who drove for a master. Bill was willing to discuss the matter *ad infinitum*, so long as the palaver was moistened by hot rum and water; but his consent was hard indeed to obtain. "I'm liable to a penalty o' five quid" was for a long time his ultimatum, — "and the forfeit o' the license besides, and you knows wot that spells, Guvnor!" But I got him round at last through a judicious appeal to the missus, whom Bill, like a good husband obeyed in all things. The missus thought the risk was nothing to speak about for the one day, "if so be that the gen'leman knows 'ow to drive." My capabilities in that regard the missus critically inspected from her open window, as I tooled the growler up and down the mews, and she was good enough to pronounce that I'd "do." So it was arranged that for a consideration I was to be virtually "Cauliflower Bill" for Christmas Day, being entitled to the use of his cab-horse, whip, cape, rugs, and badge, with the stipulation that I was on no account to approach the rank which Bill himself was in the habit of using, and where, therefore, there was a likelihood of the spurious Bill being detected.

At nine o'clock punctually I was in Bill's matrimonial bower, where I found the missus engaged in making a Christmas pudding, and Bill divided between nervousness as to our arrangement and a pint of dog-nose. My insertion into the caped cloak was the first consideration, for I happened to be a few sizes larger than Bill. But it turned out to be a garment which in effect fitted everybody, since it had no particular fit about it whatever, and I speedily found myself inside it. I cannot say that it admitted of much freedom of action in the vicinity of the biceps muscle, and it had a peculiar predilection for entangling itself in one's legs, while it was not to be disguised that it had an ancient and fish-like smell, as if it had been slept in by a horse in a state of stale perspiration. The edifice was crowned by "Cauliflower Bill's" hat, a structure of many wrinkles and much rustiness, which at once imparted to me the aspect of a rat-catcher under a cloud. Bill wrapped around my throat his voluminous comforter, in which, as it seemed, was vested the valuable property of conferring on the wearer the husky hoarseness of voice which is so characteristic of the cabman species. My legs were greaved in a pair of leathern gaiters of my own, and when I was finally made up, with whip in hand and badge on breast, the missus was pleased to say that she "wouldn't ha' knowed me from Bill hisself"—a compliment which, from such a source, was inexpressibly gratifying. I was informed by Bill that, as it was Christmas Day, he expected me to bring him home twelve shillings at the very least, and that four o'clock was the hour at which I should come back to change horses, when, said the missus, "you're 'eartily welcome to a bit o' dinner wi' me an' Bill." These preliminaries settled, I said good morning to the missus, and Bill and I turned down, and "put to."

Bill's first horse I found an uncomplaining and conscientious, but decidedly eccentric quadruped. He took a great deal of flogging, owing to the peculiarity that when you hit him only once or twice, he persisted in regarding this as a signal to fall into a walk, and had to be argued out of the error by continued applications of the short and rather inefficient whip with which Bill had provided me. Further, he never was quite happy unless when he was behind some vehicle which was proceeding at the rate of about two miles an hour, and evidently took it much to heart when compelled to pass the same. He had an unpleasant habit of lapsing into slumber whenever allowed to stand still, and in this somnolent condition would ever and anon all but tumble down, saving himself only by a scramble which was calculated to impart a nervous dread to any one interested in his welfare. Further, he had no mouth to speak of, limped all round, and had the most aggravatingly assertive stump of a tail of any horse I ever knew. But he had his virtues. He never tried to run away, and to shy on any provocation was clearly not in his nature. It was in the Camden Road where I was hailed for my first fare by a nice-looking maid-servant, who got inside and proudly rode to the house where I was to take up. My fare consisted of a young lady — a governess, probably, two chubby little girls, and a bag which obviously contained mince-pies and oranges. I was to set down at King's Cross, and I gathered from the gush of talk which preceded the final adieu that the ultimate destination of the little party was a certain aunt's house at Whetstone Park. As I drove to the station the eldest of the little maids, a bright-faced little thing, with a cataract of fair hair hanging down her back, stood up on the seat and entered into the most amusingly condescending conversation with "Mr. Cabman." She was seven last month, and her papa had given her a be-a-utiful doll that morning, and she had six Christmas cards — and please, had I got any Christmas cards? Was I to have any pudding for dinner? — she was — and had I any little girls, and did they like dolls? When I set down at the station, little Flaxenhair would have it that "Mr. Cabman" should be complimented with a mince-pie and an orange out of the paper bag. In the largeness of her heart the little one urged vigorously that to the horse also should be administered an orange, and exhibited great wonderment that the respectable quadruped — which had incontinently lapsed into slumber — was not fond of the fruit. "Not fond of oranges!" quoth little Flaxenhair, with her hands in the air, as, with a pretty nod to "Mr. Cabman," she tripped into the station.

My next fare proved the fact—if it had required proof—that all the world, even at Christmas time, does not consist of Flaxenhairs. At the foot of the Caledonian Road I was chartered by four young men, who stipulated with me that for the sum of eighteenpence and a drink I should drive them to the Manor House Tavern, Finsbury Park. They were pimply and unwholesome-looking youths, with gaudy neckties, short meerschaum pipes, and big Albert chains of a ponderosity that interfered with one's belief in their goodness. There were two "Arrys" in the quartette, and the other two went by slang nicknames. It is hardly worth while to describe them more minutely, since any one who wishes to study the genus in its most offensive development needs only to visit the "saloon" of one of the more slangy music-halls. These interesting young gentlemen smoked bad tobacco, and swore with vigor and volubility all the way to Finsbury. One of them tried as he leaned out of the cab-window to chaff a girl who was obviously on her way to church; but by the merest accident in the world, the thong of Bill's whip happened to drop rather sharply across his pimply face, which he thereupon drew in with some precipitation. I was surprised at the number of pedestrians who were tramping outward bound along the Seven Sisters' Road. In my simplicity I ascribed the concourse to the rural charms of Finsbury Park, which I remembered in the days of the great Cox to have heard conventionally spoken and written of as "one of the lungs of London." This appellation may be strictly correct, in which case I have only to remark that London has a lung which is eminently ugly, cheerless, forlorn, and generally unpleasant. There is little enough in Finsbury Park to entice a visit from any pedestrians; but it was abundantly clear that the pedestrians of the Seven Sisters' Road did not care a cent about the amenities, but had a fixed goal of some sort before their eyes, as they strode past the park-gates, and keeping to the road held on toward the Green Lanes. Beyond the tramway terminus they increased in number, so that the pavement was in a manner thronged. The outward-bound current, pushing on briskly, indeed sometimes fiercely, met the inward-bound current dawdling along more leisurely, but the people comprising the latter always gave ground deferentially to those of the former, as if recognizing their greater urgency. They were not, for the most part, wholesome-looking or creditable wayfarers who this Christmas forenoon jostled the churchgoers off the pavement of the Seven Sisters' Road. Hulking louts in moleskin and ankle-jacks, with dingy shirts open at the throat, drover young men in a quasi-Sunday attire, elegant extracts from the crowd that gathers about the head of White-friars Street when the display of a telegraphed bulletin of an important race is imminent over the way; numerous first cousins of the young gentlemen who constituted my fare — such and such like were the pedestrians we passed or met. And whither were they going or whence were they returning? To one and all there was, or had been, a common goal — the Manor House Tavern. For the thirsty souls in London there was no tap ready to flow with strong drink for the man with money in his pocket, since Christmas Day is as the Sunday to the public-houses. But a walk to the Green Lanes is held to impart the character of a *bona fide* traveller, that generally undefined and extremely vague character; and the competitive examination for admission to the alcoholic privileges of the Manor House Tavern is a very "little go" indeed. A policeman stood at the crossing over the way, no doubt charged with the duty of seeing that no actual or professing *bonâ fide* traveller was kept out of his beery birthright. Outside were drawn up some half-dozen chaises and cabs, whose inmates presumably, in the course of journeys involving issues of life and death, had succumbed to stern necessity, and had found themselves wholly unable to proceed without refreshments. The "'Arrys" and their mates alighted, and having paid me my eighteen-pence, expressed their readiness to fulfil their bargain to "stand a wet." To get in was the easiest thing in the world. The outer door was wide open, and on the door mat outside the unbolted inner door stood a mild and grinning janitor. He did not waste words by asking the applicants for admission whether they were travellers; that went without saying. "Where from?" was his simple and laconic routine-formula. "Jericho," was the response of one of the "'Arrys," with a horse-laugh, and straightway the gate of this elysium was opened unto us. The spacious bar was so crowded that it was difficult to get served, and the landlord must find much cause for self-congratulation that the spirit of exploratory enterprise is so highly developed among the inhabitants of London, more especially at hours when its guerdon is strong drink. As my fares had got into a snug corner, and appeared bent on making a forenoon of it, I started back to town empty, jogging slowly towards the Angel at Islington. As one o'clock struck, the air became full of the fragrance of baked meats. Men and children were to be seen, towels and tickets in hand, diving into the purlieus of the bake-houses, and re-emerging with baking dishes and tins, the contents of which sent forth the most appetizing odors. I had breakfasted early, and the scent kindled my hunger, so I drew on to the stand, and telling the policeman there, according to Bill's instructions, that I was going to have some refreshment, I sought the "watering-house," and found many of my brothers of the whip engaged in huge platefuls of roast pork and cabbage.

Having lunched a little less unctuously, I again mounted the box, which by this time I found becoming very hard and cramped, and jogged on towards Pentonville Hill. At the end of a street leading into the Barnsbury Road, I was hailed by a gentleman who was strictly entitled to the appellation of the head of a family. He had the family with him, as well as that fruitful vine his wife, a purposeful-looking middle-aged woman, who looked as if an odd child more or less was a trifle of which she took no account. As for the children, I absolutely decline to commit myself to statistics as to their number. They positively swarmed on and around the parent stems, so that there was no possibility of getting or keeping count of them. "Can you take the lot on us, Cabbie?" was the cheery question of the happy father of this brood. A cab has its limits of available space, and I felt scarcely justified in suggesting that the children should be packed in layers. But I left the problem to settle itself, and they all got in somehow, except the father, who rode on the box beside me, with a child in his arms that had been overlooked in the packing. Our destination was a street off the Blue Anchor Road, Bermondsey, and my box companion, who was one of the chirpiest and most laughter-loving of mortals, imparted to me the information that he and his were on their way to eat their Christmas dinner and spend the Christmas afternoon with his good lady's parents, who, it appeared, were in the tanning interest. We got so friendly that he insisted on stopping in Tooley Street and standing a quartern of gin in three "outs," one of the said "outs" being administered to the fruitful vine inside the cab. I had to push Bill's horse along the Grange Road, for my friend nourished the design of surreptitiously providing the dinner beer, and he was in dread lest the public-house should have closed before our arrival. But we were in good time. At the sound of the approaching wheels, an elderly lady, wondrous comely, spite of the atmosphere scented with odors of bone-boiling and tan-yards in which she lived, ran out, extricated a child from the cab-window before I could pull up, and was kissing it, when the living avalanche fell upon "grannie" as the cab-door was opened. My box companion had secured my co-operation in his little plot, and I crossed the street for half a gallon of "old and mild" while the family was surging in through the narrow doorway. When I returned with the drink, at the sight of which the grandparents simulated much displeased surprise, no denial was to be taken to the peremptory order that "Cabbie" was to come in and have a glass. Already the children had pervaded the house and the backyard, which latter appeared to produce a plentiful crop of cockleshells. Grandfather was at the sink in his shirt-sleeves, pouring off the water from the greens, while grandmother alternately basted a joint that hung by a worsted string before the fire, and kissed her youngest grand-infant, which she held in her lap, and whose bare bald head was so near the fire that it seemed to me that basting would have been a wise precaution with regard to it also. You should have seen the lavish way in which the dresser was decorated with evergreens, and you should have sniffed the fragrant scent which came wafted from the copper in the back kitchen, in which the pudding, securely tied in a towel, was boiling till the very moment arrived at which it should be served! It was a very humble *ménage*, but never was there better testimony to the truth of the wise man's words,—" Better is a dinner of herbs where love is, than a stalled ox and hatred therewith." Not that our friends were vegetarians—far from it; and if the beef turned out tough, I can only say that it was a very perverse and malignant proceeding on its part, in the face of the old lady's assiduity in basting. But I am sure that the beef had a better sense of the fitness of things than to do any thing of the kind.

A slow drive over the water from Bermondsey— Bill's horse appeared to go the slower the more he practised moving—brought me to the mews inhabited by "Cauliflower Bill" precisely at the hour which that worthy's good lady had stated to be their dinner time. Of the succulent fare which that estimable matron placed before her husband and myself, deigning also to partake of the same herself, I will not speak at length; yet would I breathe the secret that the unsurpassable excellence of Mrs. Cauliflower Bill's plum-pudding was imputed by herself to the circumstance that among its ingredients were minced apples and grated carrots and potatoes. When we had dined I felt at once so tired and so comfortable that I determined to forego further growler-driving, and instead accept "Cauliflower Bill" as my Gamaliel, and, sitting at his feet, listen to some of his experience in the profession. "Kebs," quoth Bill, as he drank his rum and water and whiffed at his churchwarden, "I orter know summat about kebs, I ought. I were found in the boot of a Paddington stage, an' were a parcel-boy for years afore the busses were thought on. I've druv an ackney coach and keb these height-an'-thirty year, and ain't done yet, am I, missus? Some queer things I knows consarnin' kebs, that I do. Why, there's young Billy Spriggs is married to a gal as my hold mate Tommy Toolittle found in his four-wheeler a dissolute new-born babby. It's gospel truth I'm tellin' you. Tommy took up a lady and gen'leman — quite the real toff, you know, and no gammon — in Piccadilly, and he sets 'em down at Charing Cross, an' pulls on the rank in Trafalgar Square. He 'adn't been there ten minutes when he 'ears a squallin' inside his keb, and blessed if on the mat there warn't a layin' a babby wrapped up in a red woollen shawl. In them days the shop for left property was Somerset 'Ouse, an' Tommy was on his road there with the kid, when it appeared to him as 'ow he'd better let his missus see it fust. Tommy's missus, I must tell you, never had no young 'uns of her own, an' we used to chaff Tommy cos he warn't a father. Well, Tommy's missus stripped the kid. It was dressed uncommon fine, an' wot d'ye think? — inside its roller were a twenty-pun Bank o' Hengland note. So Tommy and his missus hadopted the kid an' brought it up, and the gal turned out a good darter to 'em as ever wos, and the hold lady — Tommy's been a croaker these six year — lives along o' her an' her husband. Tommy told me how he onst reco'nized the lady as left the kid in his keb, a drivin' in a swell kerridge with a coronite on the panels and a kipple o' flunkies a hangin' on behind. He was sure she was a countess, if not a duchess, an' 'ad a mind for to follow 'er 'ome, an' see wot she was made of. But he let it alone, for by this time him an' his missus got that fond o' the young 'un, that they'd have done any thing sooner than part with it." This is a sample of "Cauliflower Bill's" gossip about his profession, which might be indefinitely prolonged, for Bill is a full reservoir of yarns, which stream out fluently the moment the sluice is raised. But there is a certain family resemblance about most of his stories, and the reader may be better content to take them as told.

THE LUCKNOW OF TO-DAY.

In the winter of 1873–4 I had gone to the East with a mission in connection with the famine which threatened the Bengal provinces so ominously, and which was fought with and worsted so gallantly by Sir Richard Temple. When his victory was assured, my work in India had ended, and it behooved me to get home again as quickly as I had gone out. But I could in no wise bring myself to quit India without first having made a pilgrimage to some of those scenes of the great Mutiny which are so many shrines for the perpetual commemoration of the heroism and constancy displayed by British men and women. For Delhi, the scene of the great siege, and the very focus of the Mutiny, it was impossible that I could spare time; but at the cost of hard and long-sustained travelling in the very hottest season of the year I was able to see Cawnpore — to stand there on the site of the memorable intrenchment, to read the inscription on the monument which covers in the " Well " — and to go on to Lucknow, the defence of whose Residency was a deed which will be remembered so long as our nation endures. To the study of Lucknow — for a study is required to master the topography of a place where so much was done — I was able to devote three whole days; and it is the results of that study which I now propose to tell.

Wandering about Cawnpore, and shutting my eyes against the architectural ambition of the Memorial Church and the leafy trimness of the Memorial Gardens, I tried hard to banish the present, made up of pleasant mess dinners, the genial sociality about the band-stand, and the grateful luxury of the club, and to recall the Cawnpore of Havelock's time. The in-marching of his little band, maddened to fury by a terrible knowledge, the straggling groups of cowering natives gazing in terror from their consciousness, too, of the awful tragedy, on the white sahibs as they tramped past, Neill's systematic enforcement of a ghastly retribution, the chivalry of the noble Outram — all these things I strove to conjure up before my mind's eye. How narrow is the boundary between tears and laughter, between the tragic and the comic! Here were men who had stood with wet eyes gazing down on an embodied tragedy, for the like of which the annals of the world may be searched in vain. The tension of the fighting had loosened, the recoil had brought despondency, and despondency had brought the swift-slaying cholera. It behooved the leaders to re-animate their men by whatever device came the readiest, and the following is a copy of an order, illustrated pictorially by the hand of a brave man who was better at fighting than at sketching: —

A Paper Hunt will take place to-morrow at half-past 5 o'clock. The meet to be at Wheler's intrenched camp.
Sept. 9, 1857.

THE LUCKNOW OF TO-DAY. 179

The envelope containing the announcement of this remarkable sporting "fixture" was addressed thus:—

Not on Her Majesty's Service.

To Adjutants of Regiments.

9th Sept.	ARTILLERY SEEN.
	1st M.F. SEEN.
	78th SEEN AND APPROVED.
For Circulation.	VOLUNTEER COMP^y do.

Take another scene. Havelock, of the serene brow, the mild blue eye, and the indomitable heart, is sitting before his tent in the short Indian twilight, that period devoted in India to the cigar and the "peg." Cigars and pegs are far from the thoughts of Havelock; he is thinking of the plight of the beleaguered ones in an exposed corner of the great city away across the Ganges in Oude, and the conversation runs wholly on this topic in the little council, whose members, besides the chief himself, are the gallant Fraser Tytler, the "boy Harry," and the devoted Harwood. Through the gloom there comes marching a file of Highlanders, escorting a tall, gaunt Oude man, on whose swarthy face the lamp-light falls as he salaams before the General Lord Sahib. He extracts from his ear a portion of quill sealed at both ends. Young Havelock opens the strange envelope, forwarded by a postal service so unique, and unrolls a morsel of paper which appears to be covered with cabalistic signs. The missive has been sent out from the general commanding the beleaguered garrison of the Lucknow Residency, and its bearer is the stanch scout Ungud. As I write, the originals of this communication and of others which came in the same way lie before me; and I give it in all its curious mixture of characters: —

Lukhnow, Septr. 16th.

My dear General, (Rec^d. 19th.)

The last letter I rec^d from you was dated 24th ult^o since when I have rec^d. νο νεως whatever from y^r. ... καμπ or of y μονεμεντς but am now δαιλη εξπεκτινγ to receive ιντελιγενσε of y^r αδνανσε in this διρεκτιον — Since the date of my last letter the enemy have continued to persevere unceasingly in their efforts against this position & the firing has never ceased day or night — they have about σιξτην guns in position round us — many of them 18 p^{rs}.? — On 5th inst. they made a very determined attack after exploding 2 mines & συκσηδεδ for a μομεντ in αλμοστ γετινγ into one of our βατεριες but were eventually repulsed on all sides with heavy loss. Since the above date they have kept up a cannonade & musketry fire, occasionally throwing in a shell or two — My ωηκλη λοσες continue very ἐνη both in οφισερς & μεν. I shall be quite out of ρυμ for the μεν in ειτ δαις, but we have been λινινγ on ρεδυσεδ ρατιωνς & I hope to be αβλε to γετ on as ... τιλ about φιρστ προξ. If you have not ρὲλιενεδ us by θ ... τιμε we shall have νο μεατ λεφτ as I must κηπ ... me few βυλοκς to μυνε my γυνς about the ποσιτιον. A's it ... I have had to κιλ almost all the γυν βυλοκς for my men c^d not περφορμ the ἀμδ ωορκ ωιθουτ ανιμαλ φοοδ. There i ... a report, tho' from a source on w^h. I

cannot implicitly rely that μαν σιυγ has just αριυεδ in λυκνοω
hav͡t λεφτ παρτ of ις φορσε ουτσιδε the σιτη. It is said that ἡ is in
ουρ ιντερεστς & that ἡ has τακεν the αβουε στεφ at the ινστιγατιον
of βριτιαh αυθοριτη. But I cannot say φορ σερταιν whether συεh
βη θη κασε or whether ἡ is ρεαλη in λυκνοω at all, as all I have to
go upon is βαζαρ ρυμουρ. I am μοστ ανξιους to ἑαρ from you of
yͬ αδυανσε to εναβλε μη to ρη-ασυρε ουρ νατιυε σολδιερς.

Yours, truly,
J. INGLIS, H.M. 32ⁿᵈ Brigadier.

To Brig! HAVELOCK, Commˢ Relieving Force.

The other missives seem to me worth printing exactly
in the manner in which they were written: —

August 16.

MY DEAR GENERAL,   (Recᵈ 23rd Augt.)

A note from Col. Tytler to Mr. Gubbins reached last
night, dated "Mungalwar, 4th instant," the latter part of
which is as follows: — "You must αιδ¹ us in ευερη way even to
cutting yͬ way out ιφ we καντ φορσε ουρ way in. We have ονλη
α σμαλλ φορσε." This has καυσεδ μη much υνεασινεσς, as it is quite
ιμποσιβλε with my ωεακ & σhατερεδ φορσε that I can λεαυε my
δεφενσες. You must bear in mind how I am αμπερεδ, that I
have upwards of ονε ἱνδρεδ & τωεντη σικ and ωουνδεδ and at the
least τωο ἱνδρεδ & τωεντη ωομεν & about τωο ἱνδρεδ & θιρτη chil-
δρεν, & no καριαγε of any δεσκριπτιον, besides σακριφισιυγ τωεντη
θρη λακς of τρεασυρε & about θιρτη γυνς of σορτς. In consequence
of the news recᵈ I shall soon put the φορσε on ἁλφ ρατιονς, unless
I ἑαρ αγαιν φρομ you. Ουρ προυισιονς will λαστ us θεν till αβουτ
the τενθ σεπτεμβερ. If you ὁπε to σαυε θισ φορσε νο τιμε μυστ be
λοστ in pushing forward. We are δαιλη being ατακεδ by the
ενεμη who are within a few yards of our δεφενσες. Their μινες
have αλρεαδη ωεακενεδ ουρ ποστ, & I have ευερη ρεασον to βελιευε
they are carrying on οθερς. Their ειγhτεεν πουνδερς are within
150 yards of σομε οφ ουρ βατεριες, & φρομ their ποσιτιον & ουρ ιναβιλιτη to φορμ ωορκινγ παρτιες, we κανοτ ρεπλι to θεμ, & ∴ θη δαμαγε

¹ The reader will observe that the words are English, though the characters are Greek.

δονε ουρλη is very γρεατ. My στρενγθ now in ευροπεανς is θρη ϋνδρεδ & φιφτη, & about θρη ϊνδρεδ νατιυες, & the men δρεαδφυλη άρασσεδ, & owing to παρτ of the ρεσιδενση having been βρουγhτ δοωn by ρουνδ σhοτ μανη are without σhελτερ. Our νατιυε φορσε hav^e been ασυρεδ on Col. Tytler's authority of y^r νεαρ απροαch σομε τωεντη φιυη δαις αγο αρε νατυραλη λοσιυγ κονφιδενσε & ιφ they λεαυε us I do not ση οω θε δεφενσες are to be μαννεδ. Did you ρεσειυε a λετερ & πλαν φρομ με φρομ θις μαν Uηjυδ? Kindly answer this question. Yours truly,

J. INGLIS.

1st September.

MY DEAR GENERAL,

Y^r letter of the 24th has duly reached me in reply to mine of 16th ult. I ρεγρετ y^r ιναβιλιτη to αδυανσε at present to ουρ ρελιεφ, but in consequence of y^r letter I have ρεδυσεδ the ρατιονς, & with this arrangement and our γρεατ δμιννυτιον ιν νυμβερς φρομ κασυαλτιες I τρυστ to be αβλε to ὁλδ ον φρομ the τωεντιθ to τωεντη φιφθ ινσταντ. Some στορες we have been ουτ οφ for the λαστ φιφτην δαις, & μανη οθερς will be εξπενδεδ before the αβουε δατε. I must be φρανκ & τελ you that my φυρσε is δαιλη δμινισhιυγ φρομ the ενεμη's μυσκετρη φιρε & ουρ δεφενσες γροω δαιλη ωεακερ. Sh^d. the ενεμη μακε α ρεαλη δετερμιυεδ εφορτ to στορμ this πλασε I shall φινδ it διφικυλτ to ρεπυλσε θεμ owing to my παυσιτη ιν νυμβερς & the ωεακ & άρασεδ στατε of the φορσε. Ουρ λοσες σινσε the κομενσεμεντ of ὁστιλιτης ἑρε have been in ευροπεανς ουλη υπωαρδς of θρη ϋνδρεδ. We are continually άράσεδ ιν κουντερμινιυγ the ενειη who have αβουτ τωεντη γυνς in ποσιτιον, μανη of λαργε καλιβ^rε. Any αδυανσε of y^{rs}. τοωαρδς θις πλασε will act βενεφισίαλη in ουρ φαυορ & γρεατλη ινσπιριτ the νατιυε παρτ of my γαρισον who ἰθερτο have βεhαυεδ λικε φαιθφυλ & γοοδ σολδιερς. If you can ποσιβλη γιυε me ανη ιντελιγενσε of y^r. ιντενδεδ αδυανσε pray do so by λετερ. Give the βεαρερ the πασσωορδ "αγρα" & ασκ ἱμ to γιυε it to μη in person. Oblige me by forwarding a copy of this letter to the G. G. I have prohibited the civil authorities from corresponding with the camp. Y^{rs}. truly,

J. INGLIS, Brig.

General HAVELOCK, Commanding Relief Force.

Copy sent to the C. O. at Allahabad for information & guidance, with the further remark that μαν σινy who was promised a jαyερ of τωo λακς κονδιτιοναλ ον his αφορδινy νο υσιστανσε to the ρεβελς is ρεπορτεδ to be στιλλ ολδινy αλοοφ & it is .˙. by no means ιμπροβαβλε that if   βαδ that Sir H. L.'s προμισε shall be κονφιρμεδ by yον' he may be ινδυσεδ to αφορδ us ακτινε ἑλπ. His φολοωερς αρε στατεδ to be σιξ θουσανδ ιν νυμβερ.

Yours truly,
2nd September.   J. INGLIS, Brigadier.

Cawnpore is an engrossing theme, and Bithoor alone would furnish material for an article; but my present subject is Lucknow, and I must get to it. There is a railway now to Lucknow from Cawnpore, but the railway bridge across the Ganges is not yet finished, and passengers must cross by the bridge of boats to the Oude side. Behind me, as the gharrie jingles over the wooden platform, is the fort which Havelock began, which Neill completed, and in which Wyndham found the shelter which alone saved him from discreditable defeat. Before me is the low Gangetic shore, with the dumpy sand-hills gradually rising from the water's edge. A few years ago there used to ride at the head of that noble regiment, the 78th Highlanders, a smooth-faced, gaunt, long-legged, stooping officer, on an old white horse. The colonel had a voice like a girl, and his men irreverently called him the "old squeaker;" but although you never heard him talk of his deeds, he had a habit of going quietly and steadily to the front, taking fighting and hardship philosophically as part of the day's work. These sand-banks were once the scene of some quiet unsensational heroism of his. He commanded the two companies of Highlanders whom Havelock threw on the unknown shore as the vanguard of his advance into Oude. No prior reconnaissance was possible. Oude swarmed with an armed and hostile population. The chances were that an army was hovering but a little way inland, waiting to attack the head of the column on landing. But it was necessary to risk all contingencies, and Mackenzie accepted the service as he might an invitation to a glass of grog. In the dead of night the boats stood across with the little forlorn hope with which Havelock essayed to grapple on to Oude. Landing in the rain and darkness, it was his work to grope for an enemy, if there should be one in his vicinity. There was not; but for four-and-twenty hours his little band hung on to the Oude bank as it were by their eyelids, detached, unsupported, and wholly charged with the taking care of themselves until it was possible to send a re-enforcement. The charge of this vague, uncertain, tentative enterprise, fraught with risks so imminent and so vast, required a cool, steady-balanced courage of no common order.

"Onao!" shouts the conductor of the train at the first station from Cawnpore, and we look out on a few railway bungalows, and a large native village apparently in a ruinous state. All this journey is studded with battle-fields, and this is one of them. If I had time I should like to make a pilgrimage to the street mouth into which dashed frantically Private Patrick Cavanagh of the 64th, stung to madness by the hesitation of his fellows, and was cut to pieces by the tulwars of the mutineers. We jog on very slowly: the Oude and Rohilcund Railway is to India in point of slowness what the Great Eastern is to us; but every yard of the ground is interesting. Along that *chaussée* passed in long, strangely diversified procession the people whom Clyde brought away from Lucknow — the civilians, the women, and the children and the wounded of the immortal garrison. That swell beyond the mango trees, under which the *nhil gau* are feeding, is Mungalwar, Havelock's menacing position. No wonder though the outskirts of this town on the high road present a ruined appearance. It is Bussecrutgunge, the scene of three of Havelock's battles and victories, fought and won in a single fortnight. We pass Bunnee, where Havelock and Outram, tramping on to the relief, fired a royal salute in the hope that the sound of it might reach to the Residency and cheer the hearts of its garrison. And now we are on the platform of the Lucknow station, which has more of an English look about it than have most Indian stations. There is a bookstall, although it is not one of Smith's; and there are lots of English faces in the crowd waiting the arrival of the train. The natives, one sees at a glance, are of very different physique from the people of Bengal. The Oude man is tall, square-shouldered, and upright; he has more hair on his face than has the Bengali, and his carriage is that of a free man. The railway station of Lucknow is flanked by two earthwork fortifications of considerable pretensions.

Lucknow is so full of interest, and the objects of interest are so widely spread, that one is in doubt where to begin the pilgrimage. But the Alumbagh is on the railway side of the canal, and therefore nearest; and I drive directly to it before going into the town. From the station the road to the Alumbagh turns sharp to the left, and the two miles' drive is through beautiful groves and gardens. Then the plain opens up, and there is the detached temple which so long was one of Outram's outlying pickets; and to the left of it the square walled enclosure of the Alumbagh itself, with the four corners flanked by earthen bastions. The top of the wall is everywhere roughly crenellated for musketry fire, and on two of its faces there are countless tokens that it has been the target for round shot and bullets. The Alumbagh in the pre-Mutiny period was a pleasure-garden of one of the princes of Oude. The enclosed park contained a summer palace, and all the surroundings were pretty and tasteful. It was for the possession of the Alumbagh that Havelock fought his last battle before the relief; here it was where he left his baggage when he went in; here it was that Clyde halted to organize the turning movement which achieved the second relief. Hither were brought from the Dilkoosha the women and children of the garrison, prior to starting on the march for Cawnpore; here Outram lay threatening Lucknow from Clyde's relief until his ultimate capture of the city. But these occurrences contribute but trivially to the interest of the Alumbagh in comparison with the circumstance that within its enclosure is the grave of Havelock. We enter it under the lofty arch of the castellated gateway. From this a straight avenue, bordered by *arbor vitæ* trees, conducts to a square plot of ground, enclosed by low posts and chains. Inside this there is a little garden, the plants of which a native gardener is watering as we open the wicket. From the centre of the little garden there rises a shapely obelisk on a square pedestal, and on one side of the pedestal is a long inscription. "Here lie," it begins, "the mortal remains of Henry Havelock;" and so, methinks, it might have ended. There is needed no prolix biographical inscription to tell the reverent pilgrim of the deeds of the dead man by whose grave he stands — so long as history lives, so long does it suffice to know that " here lie the mortal remains of Henry Havelock " — and the text and verse of poetry grate on one as redundancies. He sickened two days before the evacuation of the Residency, and died on the morning of the 24th, in his dhooly, in a tent of the camp at the Dilkoosha. The life went out of him just as the march began, and his soldiers conveyed with them, on the litter on which he had expired, the mortal remains of the noble chief who had so often led them on to victory.

The same afternoon they buried him here under the tree which still spreads its branches over the little garden in which he lies. There stood around the grave mouth Campbell, and the chivalrous Outram, and stanch old Walter Hamilton, and the ever-ready Fraser Tytler; and the " boy Harry," to whom the campaign had brought the gain of fame and the loss of a father; and the devoted Harwood, with " his heart in the coffin there with Cæsar; " and the heroic William Peel; and that " colossal red Celt," the noble, ill-fated Adrian Hope, sacrificed afterwards to incompetent obstinacy. Behind stood in a wide circle the soldiers of the " Ross-shire Buffs," and the " Blue Caps," who had served him so stanchly, and had gathered here now, with many a memory of his ready praise of valor, and his indefatigable regard for the comfort of his men, stirring in their war worn hearts: —

> Guarded to a soldier's grave
> By the bravest of the brave,

> He hath gained a nobler tomb
> Than in old cathedral gloom.
> Nobler mourners paid the rite
> Than the crowd that craves a sight;
> England's banners o'er him waved,
> Dead he keeps the name he saved.

The place was being temporarily abandoned, and as the rebels desecrated all the graves they could discover, it was necessary to obliterate as much as possible the tokens of the interment. A big "H" was carved into the bark of the tree, and a small tin plate fastened to its trunk, to guide to the subsequent investigation of the spot. Dr. Russell tells us that when he visited the Alumbagh before his return home after the mutiny in Oude was stamped out, he found the hero's grave a muddy trench near the foot of a tree which bore the mark of a round shot and had carved into its bark the letter "H." The tree is here still and the dent of the round shot, and faintly too, is to be discerned the carved letter, but the bark around it seems to have been whittled away, perhaps by the sacrilegious knives of relic-seeking visitors. There is the grave of a young lieutenant in a corner of the little garden, and a few private soldiers lie hard by.

I turn my face now toward the Charbagh bridge, following the route taken by Havelock's force on the memorable day of the relief. There is the field where, as, at a table in the open air, Havelock and Outram were studying a map, a round shot from the Sepoy battery by the Yellow House ricochetted over them. There is the spot where stood the Yellow House itself, whence after a desperate struggle Maud's artillerymen drove the garrison and the guns. And now with a sweep the road comes into a direct line with the Charbagh bridge over the canal. Now there is not a house in the vicinity; the Charbagh garden has been thrown into the plain, and the steep banks of the canal are perfectly naked. But then the scene was very different. On the Lucknow side the native city came close up to the bridge and lined the canal. The tall houses to right and left of the bridge on the Lucknow side were full of men with fire-arms. At that end of the bridge there was a regular overlapping breastwork, and behind it rose an earthwork battery solidly constructed, and armed with six guns, one a 42-pounder, all crammed to the muzzle with grape. Let us sit down on the parapet and try to realize the scene. Outram with the 78th has made a detour to the right through the Charbagh garden to clear it of the enemy, and, gaining the canal bank, to bring a flanking fire to bear on its defenders. There is only room for two of Maud's guns, and there they stand out in the open on the road trying to answer the fire of the rebel battery. Thrown forward along the bank to the left of the bridge is a company of the Madras Fusiliers under Arnold, lying down, and returning the musketry fire from the houses on the other side. Maud's guns are forward in the straight throat of the road where it leads on to the bridge close by, but round the bend under the cover of the wall the Madras Fusiliers are lying down. In a bay of the wall of the Charbagh enclosure General Neill is standing, waiting for the effect of Outram's flank movement to develop, and young Havelock, mounted, is on the other side of the road somewhat forward. Matters are at a dead lock. It seems as if Outram had lost his way. Maud's gunners are all down, he has repeatedly called for volunteers from the infantry behind, and now he and his subaltern, Maitland, are each doing bombardier's work. Maud calls to young Havelock that he shall be forced to retire his guns if nothing is done at once, and Havelock rides across through the fire, and in his capacity of assistant adjutant-general urges on Neill the need for an immediate assault. Neill " is not in command; he cannot take the responsibility; and General Outram must turn up soon." Havelock turns and rides away down the road, towards the rear. As he passes he speaks encouragingly to the recumbent Fusiliers, who are getting fidgety at the long detention under fire, " Come out of that, sir," cries one soldier, " a chap's just had his head taken off there!" It is a grim joke that reply which tickles the Fusiliers into laughter: " And what the devil are we here for but to get our heads taken off?" Young Havelock is bent on the perpetration of what under the circumstances may be called a pious fraud. His father, who commands the operations, is behind with the reserve, and he disappears round the bend on the make-belief of getting instructions from the chief. The general is far in the rear, but his son comes back at the gallop, rides up to Neill, and saluting with his sword, says, " You are to carry the bridge at once, sir." Neill, acquiescing in the superior order, replies, " Get the regiment together then, and see it formed up." At the word, and without waiting for the regiment to rise and form, the gallant and eager Arnold springs up from his advanced position and dashes on to the bridge, followed by about a dozen of his nearest skirmishers. Tytler and Havelock, as eager as Arnold, set spurs to their horses, and are by his side in a moment. Then the hurricane opens. The big gun, crammed to the muzzle with grape, sweeps its iron sleet across the bridge in the face of the gallant band, and the Sepoy sharpshooters converge their fire on it. Arnold drops shot through both thighs. Tytler and his horse go down with a crash, the bridge is swept clear save for Havelock, erect and unwounded, waving his sword and shouting for the Fusiliers to come on, and a Fusilier corporal, Jakes by name, who, as he rams a bullet home into his Enfield, says cheerily to Havelock, "We'll soon have the —— out of that, sir!" And corporal Jakes is a true prophet. Before the big gun can be loaded again the Fusiliers are on the bridge in a rushing mass. They are across it, they clear the barricade, they storm the battery, they are bayonetting the Sepoy gunners as they stand. The Charbagh bridge is won, but with severe loss, which continues more or less all the way to the Residency; and when one comes to know the ground it becomes more and more obvious that the strategy of Havelock, overruled by Outram, was wise and prescient, when he counselled a wide turning movement by the Dilkoosha, over the Goomtee near the Martiniere, and so along its northern bank to the Badshah-bagh, almost opposite to the Residency and commanding the iron bridge.

I recross the Charbagh bridge, and bend away to the left by the by-road along the canal side which Havelock followed. Several roads are open to me, but I follow that by which the 78th Highlanders penetrated to the front of the Kaiser-bagh. Most of the native houses are now destroyed, whence was poured so deadly a fire on the advancing Ross-shire men that three color-bearers fell in succession, and the color fell to the grasp of the gallant Valentine M'Master, the assistant-surgeon of the regiment. And now I stand in front of the main entrance to the Kaiser-bagh, hard by the spot where stood the Sepoy battery which the Highlanders so opportunely took in reverse. Before me on the *maidan* is the plain monument to Sir Mountstuart Jackson, Captain Orr, and a sergeant, who were murdered in the Kaiser-bagh when the success of Campbell's final operations became certain. I enter the great square enclosure of the Kaiser-bagh, and stand in the desolation of what was once a gay garden where the King of Oude and his women were wont to disport themselves. The place stands much as Campbell's men left it after looting its multifarious rich treasures. The dainty little pavilions are empty and dilapidated, the statues are broken and tottering. Quitting the Kaiser-bagh, I try to realize the scene of that informal council of war in one of the outlying court-yards of the numerous palaces. I want to fix the spot where, on his big waler sat Outram, a splash of blood across his face, and his arm in a sling; where Havelock, dismounted, walked up and down by Outram's side with short nervous strides, halting now and then to give emphasis to the argument, while all around them were officers, soldiers, guns, natives, wounded men, bullocks, and a surging tide of disorganization momentarily pouring into the square. But the attempt is fruitless. The whole area has been cleared of buildings right up to the gate of the Residency, only that hard by the Goomtee there still stands the river wing of the Chutter Munzil Palace, with its fantastic architecture, and the Palace of the Kings of Oude is now the Station Library and Assembly Rooms. The Hureen Khana, the Lallbagh, the courts of the Furrut Bux Palace, the Khas Bazaar, and the Clock Tower have alike been swept away; and in their place there opens up before the eye trim ornamental grounds, with neat plantations which extend up to the Bailey-guard gate itself. One archway alone stands — a gaunt commemorative skeleton — a pedestal for the statue of a noble soldier. It was from a chamber above the crown of this arch that the Sepoy shot Neill as he sat on his horse urging the confused press of guns and men through the archway. The spot is memorable for other causes. This archway led into that court which is world-famous under the name of Dhooly Square. Here it was where the bearers abandonded the wounded in the dhoolies which poor Bensley Thornhill was trying to guide into the Residency; here it was where they were butchered and burned as they lay, and here it was where Dr. Home and a handful of men of the escort did what in them lay to cover the wounded, and defended themselves for a day and a night against continuous attacks of countless enemies.

The *via dolorosa*, the road of death up which Outram and Havelock fought their way with Brazier's Sikhs and the Ross-shire Buffs, is now a pleasant open drive amid clumps of trees, leading on to the Residency. A strange thrill runs through my frame as there opens up before me that reddish gray crumbling archway spanning the road. Its face is dented and splintered with cannon-shot. and pitted all over by musket-bullets.

This is none other than that historic Bailey-guard gate which burly Jock Aitken and his faithful Sepoys kept so stanchly. You may see the marks still of the earth banked up against it on the interior during the siege. To the right and left runs the low wall which was the curtain of the defence, now crumbled so as to be almost indistinguishable. But there still stands, retired somewhat from the right of the archway, Aitken's post — the guard-house and treasury, its pillars and façade cut and dented all over with the marks of bullets fired by "Bob the Nailer" and his comrades from the Clock Tower which stood over against it. And in the curtain wall between the archway and the building, is still to be traced the faint outline of the embrasure through which Outram and Havelock entered on the memorable evening. The turmoil and din and conflicting emotions of that terrible. glorious day have merged into a strange serenity of quietude. The scene is solitary, save for a native woman who is playing with her baby on a spot where once dead bodies lay in heaps. But the other scene rises up vividly before the mind's eye out of the present calm. Havelock and Outram and the staff have passed through the embrasure here, and now there are rushing in the men of the ranks, powder-grimed, dusty, bloody; but a minute before raging with the stern passion of the battle, now full of a womanlike tenderness. And all around them, as they swarm in, there crowd a mass of folk eager to give welcome. There are officers and men of the garrison, civilians whom the siege has made into soldiers; women, too, weeping tears of joy down on the faces of the children for whom they had not dared to hope for aught but death. There are gaunt men, pallid with loss of blood, whose great eyes shine weirdly amid the torch-light, and whose thin hands tremble with weakness as they grip the sinewy, grimy hands of the Highlanders. These are the wounded of the long siege, who have crawled out from the hospital up yonder, as many of them as could compass the exertion, with a welcome to their deliverers. The hearts of the impulsive Highlanders wax very warm. As they grasp the hands held out to them, they exclaim, "God bless you!" "Why, we expected to have found only your bones!" "And the children are living too!" and many other fervid and incoherent ejaculations. The ladies of the garrison come among the Highlanders, shaking them enthusiastically by the hand; and the children clasp the shaggy men round the neck, and, to say truth, so do some of the mothers. But Jessie Dunbar and her "Dinna ye hear it?" in reference to the bagpipe music, are in the category of melodramatic fictions.

The position which bears and will bear to all time the title of the Residency of Lucknow is an elevated plateau of land, irregular in surface, of which the highest point was occupied by the Residency building, while the area around was studded irregularly with buildings, chiefly the houses of the principal civilian officials of the station. When Campbell brought away the garrison in November, 1857, it lapsed into the hands of the mutineers, who held it till his final occupation of the city and its surroundings in March of the following year. They pulled down not a few of the already shattered buildings, and left their fell imprint on the spot in an atrociously ghastly way by desecrating the graves in which brave hands had laid our dead country-people, and flinging the exhumed corpses into the Goomtee. When India once more became settled, the Residency, its commemorative features uninterfered with, was laid out as a garden, and flowers and shrubs now grow on soil once wet with the blood of heroes. The *débris* has been removed or dispersed; the shattered buildings are prevented from crumbling further; tablets bearing the names of the different positions and places of interest are let into the walls; and it is possible, by exploring the place map in hand, to identify all the features of the defence. The avenue from the Bailey-guard gate rises with a steep slope to the Residency building. On either side of the approach, and hard by the gate, are the blistered and shattered remnants of two large houses: that on the right is the banqueting house, which was used as the hospital during the siege; that on the left was Dr. Fayrer's house. The banqueting house is a mere shell, riven everywhere with shot, and pitted over by musket-bullets, as if it had suffered from small-pox. The ground-floor has escaped with less damage, but the banqueting hall itself has been wholly wrecked by the persistent fire which the rebels showered upon it, and to which, notwithstanding the mattresses and sand-bags with which the windows were blocked, several poor fellows fell victims as they lay wounded on their cots. Dr. Fayrer's house is equally a battered ruin. In its first floor, roofless and forlorn, its front torn open by shot, and the pillars of its window jagged into fantastic fragments, is the room in which Sir Henry Havelock died, exposed to fire to the very last. At the top of the slope of the avenue, and on the left front of the Residency building as we approach it — on what, indeed, was once the lawn — has been raised an artificial mound, its slopes covered with flowering shrubs, its summit bearing the monumental obelisk, on the pedestal of which is the terse, appropriate inscription: — "In memory of Major-General Sir Henry Lawrence and the brave men who fell in defence of the Residency. *Si monumentum quaeris Circumspice!*" Beyond this lies the scathed and blighted ruin of the Residency House, once a large and imposing structure, now so utterly wrecked and shivered, that one wonders how the crumbling reddish gray walls are kept erect. The veranda was battered down, and much of the front of the building lies bodily open, the structure being supported on the battered and distorted pillars, assisted by great baulks of wood. Entering by the left wing, I pass down a winding stair into the bowels of the earth, till I reach the spacious and lofty vaults or *tykhana* under the building. Here, the place affording comparative safety, lived immured the women of the garrison, the soldiers' wives, half-caste females, the wives of the meaner civilians, and their children. The poor creatures were seldom allowed to come up to the surface, lest they should come in the way of the shot which constantly lacerated the whole area, and few visitors were allowed access to them. Veritably they were in a dungeon. Provisions were lowered down to them from the window orifices near the roof of the vaulting, and there were days when the firing was so heavy that orders were given to them not even to rise from their beds on the floor. For shot occasionally found a way even into the *tykhana;* you may see the holes it made in penetrating. The miserables were billeted off ten in a room, and there they lived, without sweepers, baths, dhobies, or any of the comforts which the climate makes necessities. Here in these dungeons children were born, only for the most part to die. Ascending another staircase I pass through some rooms in which lived (and died) some of the ladies of the garrison, and passing from the left wing by a shattered corridor, am able to look up into the room in which Sir Henry Lawrence received his death wound. Access to it is impossible by reason of the tottering condition of the structure; and turning away I clamber up the worn staircase in the shot-riven tower, on the summit of which still stands the flagstaff on which were hoisted the signals with which the garrison were wont to communicate with the Alumbagh. The walls of the staircase and the flat roof of the tower are scratched and written all over with the names of visitors; many of the names are those of natives, but more are those of British soldiers, who have occasionally added a piece of their mind in characteristically strong language.

I set out on a pilgrimage under the still easily traceable contour of the intrenchment. Passing "Sam Lawrence's Battery" above what was the water gate, I traverse the projecting tongue at the end of which stood the "Redan Battery," whose fire swept the river face up to the iron bridge. Returning, and passing the spot where "Evans's Battery" stood, I find myself in the churchyard, in a slight depression of the ground. Of the church, which was itself a defensive post, not one stone remains on another, and the mutineers hacked to pieces the ground of the churchyard. The ground is now neatly enclosed and ornamentally planted, and is studded with many monuments, few of which speak the truth when they profess to cover the dust of those whom they commemorate. There are the regimental monuments of the 5th Madras Fusiliers, the 84th (360 men besides officers), the Royal Artillery, the 90th (a long list of officers and 271 men). The monument of the 1st Madras Fusiliers bears the names of Neill, Stephenson, Renaud, and Arnold, and commemorates a loss of 352 men. There is a monument to Mr. Polehampton, the exemplary chaplain, and hard by a plain slab bears the inscription, "Here lies Henry Lawrence, who tried to do his duty: may the Lord have mercy on his soul!" words dictated by himself on his death-bed. Other monuments commemorate Captain Graham of the Bengal Cavalry and two children, Mr. Fairhurst, the Roman Catholic chaplain, Major Banks, Captain Fulton, of the 32nd, who earned the title of "defender of Lucknow;" Lucas, the travelling Irish gentleman, who served as a volunteer, and fell in the last sortie; Captain Becher, Captain Moorsom, poor Bensley Thornhill, and his young daughter, "Mrs. Elizabeth Arne, burnt with a shell-ball during the siege," Lieutenant Cunliffe, Mr. Ommaney the Judicial Commissioner, and others. The nameless hillocks of poor Jack Private are plentiful, for here were buried many of those who fell in the final capture; and there are children's graves. Interments take place still. I saw a freshly-made grave; but only those are entitled to a last resting-place here who were among the beleaguered during the long defence. I have seen the medal for the defence of Lucknow on the bosom of a man who was a child in arms at the time of the siege. and such an one would have the right to claim interment in this doubly hallowed ground. From the churchyard I pass out along the narrow neck to that forlorn-hope post, "Innes' Garrison," and along the western face of the intrenchment by the sides of the sheep-house and the slaughter, to Gubbins's post. The mere foundations of the house are visible which the stout civilian so gallantly defended, and the famous tree, gradually pruned to a mere stump by the enemy's fire, is no longer extant. Along the southern face of the position there are no buildings which are not ruined. Sikh Square, the Brigade Mess House, and the Martinière boys' post, are alike represented by fragmentary gray walls, shivered with shot, and shored up here and there by beams. The rooms of the Begum Kothi, near the centre of the position, are still laterally entire, but roofless. The walls of this structure are exceptionally thick, and here many of the ladies of the garrison were quartered. All around the Residency position the native houses, which at the time of the siege crowded close up on the intrenchment, are now destroyed; and, indeed, the native town has been curtailed into comparatively small dimensions, and is entirely separated from the area in which the houses of the station are built.

Quitting the Residency, I drive westward by the river side, over the site of the Captan Bazaar, past the iron bridge and the Nawab's bridge, past also that huge fortified heap the Muchee Bawn, till I reach the beautiful enclosure in which the great Inambara stands. This majestic structure — part temple, part convent, part palace, and now part fortress — dominates the whole terrain, and from its lofty flat roof one looks down on the plain, where the weekly *hát* or market is being held, on the gardens and mansions across the river, and southward upon the dense mass of houses which constitute the native city. Sentries promenade the battlements of the Muchee Bawn and the Inambara, and batteries of great guns frown out across the cleared plain on the city. The great Hall of the Inambara — an apartment to which, for space and height, I know none in Europe comparable — is now used as an arsenal, and here are stored the great siege guns which William Peel plied with so great skill and gallantry. Just outside the Inambara, on the edge of the *maidan* between it and the Moosabagh, I come on a little railed churchyard, where rest a few British soldiers who fell during Lord Clyde's final operations in this direction. Then, with a sweep across the plain to the south, and by a slight ascent, I reach the gate of the city which opens into the *Chowk* or principal street — the street traversed in disguise by the dauntless Kavanagh when he went out from the garrison to convey information, and afford guidance to Sir Colin Campbell on his first advance. The gate-house is held by a strong force of native policemen, armed as if they were soldiers; and as I pass the guard I stand in the *Chowk* itself, in the midst of a throng of gayly clad male pedestrians, women in chintz trousers, laden donkeys, multitudinous children, and still more multitudinous stinks. All down both sides, the fronts of the lower stories are open, and in the recesses sit merchants displaying paltry jewelry, slippers, pipes, turban cloths, and Manchester stuffs of the gaudiest patterns. The main street of Lucknow has been called "The Street of Silver," but I could find little among its jewelry either of silver or of gold. The first floors all have balconies, and on these sit draped barefooted women of Rahab's profession. The women of Lucknow are fairer and handsomer, and the men bolder and more stalwart, than in Bengal; and it takes no great penetration to discern that Lucknow is still ruled by fear, and not by love.

It remained for me still to investigate the scenes of the route by which Lord Clyde came in on both his advances; but to do justice to these would demand separate articles. Let me begin the hasty sketch at the Dilkoosha Palace, two miles and more away to the east of the Residency; for on both occasions the Dilkoosha was Clyde's base. Wajid Ali's twenty-foot wall has now given place to an earthen embankment surrounding a beautiful pleasure park, and there are now smooth green slopes instead of the dense forest through which Clyde's soldiers marched on their turning movement. On a swell in the midst of the park, commanding a view of the fantastic architecture of the Martiniere down by the tank, stands the gaunt ruin of the once trim and dainty Dilkoosha Palace, or rather garden house. From one of the pepper-box turrets up there Lord Clyde directed the attack on the Martiniere in his ultimate operation; and here it was that, as Dr. Russell tells us, a round shot dispersed his staff on the adjacent leads. After quietude was restored the Dilkoosha was the head-quarters for a time of Sir Hope Grant, but now it has been allowed to fall into decay, although the garden in the rear of it is prettily kept up. On the reverse slope behind the Dilkoosha, was the camp in one of the tents of which Havelock died. We drive down the gentle slope once traversed at a rushing double by the Black Watch on their way to carry the Martiniere, past the great tank, out of the centre of which rises the tall column to the memory of Claude Martine, and reach the entrance of the fantastic building which he built, in which he was buried, and which bears his name. We see at the angle of the northern wing the slope up which the gun was run which played so heavily on the Dilkoosha up on the wooded knoll there. The Martiniere is now, as it was before the Mutiny, a college for European boys, and the young fellows are playing on the terraces. Grotesque stone statues are in niches and along the tops of the balconies; you may see on them the marks of the bullets which the honest fellows of the Black Watch fired at them, taking them for Pandies. I go down into a vault, and see the tomb of Claude Martine; but it is empty, for the mutineers desecrated his grave, and scattered his bones to the winds of heaven. Then I make for the roof, through the dormitories of the boys, and past fantastic stone griffins and lions and Gorgons, till I reach the top of the tower, and touch the flagstaff from which in the relief was given the answering signal to that hoisted on the tower of the Residency. I stand in the niches where the mutineer marksmen used to sit with their hookahs, and take pot shots at the Dilkoosha. I look down to the eastward on the Goomtee, and note the spot where Outram crossed on that flank movement which would have been so much more successful than it was had he been permitted to drive it home. To the north-east, beyond the topes, is the battle-ground of Chinhut, where Lawrence received so terrible a reverse at the beginning of the siege. Due north is the Koodrail viaduct, which Outram cleared with the Rifles and the 79th, and in whose vicinity Jung Bahadour, the crafty and bloodthirsty generalissimo of Nepaul, "co-operated" by a demonstration, which never became any thing more. And to the west there lie stretched out before me the domes, minarets, and spires of Lucknow, rising above the foliage in which their bases are hidden; and the routes of Clyde in the relief and the capture. The rays of the afternoon sun are stirring into color the dusky gray of the Secunderbagh, and of the Nuddun Rusoot, or "Grave of the Prophet," used as a powder magazine by the rebels. Below me on the lawn of the Martiniere is the big gun — one of Claude Martine's casting — which did the rebels so much service at the other angle of the Martiniere, and which was spiked at last by two of Peel's naval brigade, who swam the Goomtee for the purpose. That little enclosure slightly to the left front surrounds "all that can die" of that strange mixture of high spirit, cool daring, and weak principle, the famous chief of Hodson's Horse. By Hodson's side lies Captain da Costa of the 56th N. I., attached to Brazier's Sikhs. Of this officer is told that, having lost many relatives in the butchery of Cawnpore, he joined the regiment likeliest to be in the front of the Lucknow fighting, and fell by one of the first shots fired in the assault on the Kaiser-bagh.

Descending from the Martiniere tower, I traverse the park to the westward, passing the grave of Captain Otway Mayne, cross the dry canal, along which are still visible the heaps of earth which mark the stupendous first line of the rebels' defences, and bending to the left reach the Secunderbagh. This famous place was a pleasure garden surrounded with a lofty wall, with turrets at the angles and a castellated gateway. The interior garden is now waste and forlorn, the rank grass growing breast-high in the corners where the slaughter was heaviest. Here in this little enclosure, not bigger than the garden of Bedford Square, 2,000 Sepoys died the death at the hands of the 93rd, the 53rd, and the 4th Punjaubees. Their common grave is under the low mound on the other side of the road. The loopholes stand as they were left by the mutineers when our fellows came bursting in through the ragged breach made in the reverse side from the main entrance by Peel's guns. Further on — that is nearer to the Residency — I come to the Shah Nujeef, with its strong exterior wall enclosing the domed temple in its centre. It is still easy to trace the marks of the breach made in the angle of the wall by Peel's battering guns, and the tree is still standing up which Salmon, Southwell, and Harrison climbed in response to his proffer of the Victoria Cross. Opposite the Shah Nujeef white girls are playing on the lawn of that castellated building, for the Koorsheyd Munzil, on the top of which Garnet Wolseley hoisted the British flag in the face of a *feu d'enfer*, is now a seminary for the daughters of Europeans. A little beyond, on the plain in front of the Motee Mahal, is the spot where Campbell met Outram and Havelock, — a spot which, methinks, might well be marked by a monument; and after this I lose my reckoning by reason of the extent of the demolition, and am forced to resort to guess-work as to the precise localities.

RAILWAY LIZZ.

BY AN HOSPITAL SISTER.

We see many curious phases of humanity — we who administer to the sick in the great hospitals which are among the boasts of London. The mask worn by the face of the world is dropped before us. We see men as they are, and while the sight is often not calculated to enhance our estimate of human nature, there are occasionally strong reliefs which stand out from the mass of shadow. There are curious opinions entertained in the outer world as to the internal economy of hospitals, not a few "laymen" imagining that the main end of such establishments is that the doctors may have something to experiment upon for the advancement of their professional theories — something which, while it is human, is not very valuable in the social scale, and therefore open to be hacked and hewn and operated upon with a freedom begotten of the knowledge that the subject is a mere *vile corpus*.

Nor is this the only delusion. Many people think that the hospital nurse is but another name for a heartless harpy, brimful of callous selfishness, and sodden with ill-gotten gin. Her attentions — kindness is an inadmissible word — are believed to be purely mercenary. Those who themselves can afford to fee her, or who have friends able and willing to buy her services, may purchase civil treatment and careful nursing, while the poor wretch who has neither money nor friends may languish unheeded. There is no greater mistake than this. Year by year the character of hospital nursing is improving. It is not to be denied that in times gone by there were nurses the mainsprings of whose actions may be said to have been money and gin; but these have long since been driven forth with contumely. I have seen a poor wretch of a discharged soldier, without a single copper to bless himself with, nursed with as much tender assiduity and real feeling as if he were in a position to pay his nurses handsomely.

Indeed, in most hospitals now the practice of accepting money presents is altogether forbidden; and if the prohibition, as in the case of railway porters and guards, is sometimes looked upon in the light of a dead letter, there is, I sincerely believe, no such thing as any grasping after a guerdon, or any neglect in a case where it is evident no guerdon is to be expected. There is an hospital I could name in which the nurses are prohibited from accepting from patients any more substantial recognition of their services than a nosegay of flowers. The wards of this hospital are always gay with bright, fragrant posies, most of them the contributions of those who, having been carefully tended in their need, retain a grateful recollection of the kindness, and now that they are in health again, take this simple, pretty way of showing their gratitude. It is two years ago since a rough bricklayer's laborer got mended in the accident ward of this hospital of some curiously-complicated injuries he had received by tumbling from the top of a house. Not a Sunday afternoon has there been since the house-surgeon told him one morning he might go out, that he has not religiously revisited the "Albert" ward, and brought his thanks-offering in the shape of a cheap but grateful nosegay.

Those nurses who thus devote themselves to the tending of sick, have often curious histories if anybody would be at the trouble of collecting them. It is not always mere regard for the securing of the necessaries of life which has brought them to the thankless and toilsome occupation. We have all read of nunneries in which women immured themselves, anxious to sequester themselves from all association with the outer world, and to devote themselves to a life of penance and devotion. After all, their piety was aimless, and of no utility to humanity. There was a concentrated selfishness in it which detracted from its ambitious aspiration. But in the modern nuns of our hospitals methinks we have women who, abnegating with equal solicitude the pleasures and dissipations of the world, find a more philanthropic opening for their exertions in their retirement than in sleeping on hair pallets, and eating nothing but parched peas.

It was towards the autumn of last year that a modest-looking young woman applied to me for a situation on our nursing staff. She wore a widow's dress, and seemed a self-contained, reserved little woman, with something weighing very heavily on her mind. Her testimonials of character were ample and of a very high order, but they did not enlighten me with any great freedom as to her past history, and she for her part appeared by no means eager to supplement the meagre information furnished by them. However, people have a right to keep their own counsel if they please, and there was no sin in the woman's reticence.

We happened to be very short of efficient nurses at the time, and she was at once taken upon trial; her somewhat strange stipulation, which she made absolute, being agreed to — that she should not be compelled to reside in the hospital, but merely to come in to perform her turn of nursing, and that over, be at liberty to leave the precincts when she pleased. I say the stipulation was a strange one, because attached to it there was a considerable pecuniary sacrifice, as well as a necessity for entering a lower grade.

She made a very excellent nurse, with her quiet, reserved ways, and her manner of moving about a ward as if she studied the lightness of every footfall. But she had her peculiarities. I have already said she was not given to be communicative, and for the first three months she was in the place, I do not believe she uttered a word to any one within the walls, except on subjects connected with the performance of her duties. Then, too, she manifested a curious fondness for being on duty in the accident ward. Most nurses have very little liking for this ward — the work is very heavy and unremitting, and frequently the sights are more than usually repulsive. But she specially made application to be placed in it, and the more terrible the nature of the accident, the more eager was her zeal to minister to the poor victim. It seemed almost a morbid fondness which she developed for waiting, in particular, upon people injured by railway accidents. When some poor mangled plate-layer, or a railway-porter crushed almost out of resemblance to humanity, would be borne in, and laid on an empty cot in the accident ward, this woman was at the bedside with a seeming intuitive perception of what would best conduce to soothe and ease the poor shattered wretch, and she would wait on him "hand and foot" with an intensity of devotion far in excess of what mere duty, however conscientiously fulfilled, would have demanded of her. Indeed, her partiality for railway "cases" was so marked, that it appeared to amount to a passion; and among the other nurses, never slow to fix upon any peculiarity, and base upon it some not unkindly nickname, our quiet friend went by the name of "Railway Lizz." Nobody ever got any clew to the reason, if there was one, for this *penchant* of hers. Indeed, nobody ever was favored with the smallest scrap of her confidence. I confess to have felt much interest in the sad-eyed young widow, and to have several times given her an opening which she might have availed herself of for narrating something of her past life; but she always retired within herself with a sensitiveness which puzzled me not a little, satisfied as I was that there was nothing in her antecedents of a character which would not bear the light.

There are no holidays within an hospital. Physical suffering is not to be mitigated by a gala day; the pressure of disease cannot be lightened by jollity and merry-making. On New Year's Eve, when the world outside our walls was glad of heart, a poor shattered form was borne into the accident ward. It was a railway-porter, whom a train had knocked down and passed over, crushing the young fellow almost out of the shape of humanity. Railway Lizz was by his side in a moment, wetting the pain-parched lips, and smoothing the pillow of the half-conscious sufferer. The house-surgeon came and went with that silent shake of the head we know too surely how to interpret, and the mangled railway-porter was left in the care of his assiduous nurse. It was almost midnight when I again entered the accident ward. The night-lamp was burning feebly, shedding a dim dull light over the great room, and throwing out huge grotesque shadows on the floor and the walls. I glanced toward the railway-porter's bed, and the tell-tale screen placed around it told me that all was over, and that the life had gone out of the shattered casket. As I walked down the room toward it, I heard a low subdued sound of bitter sobbing behind it, and when I stepped within it, there was the sad-faced widow-nurse weeping as if her heart would break. When she saw me, she strove hard to repress her emotion, and resume the quiet, self-possessed demeanor which it was her wont to wear; but she failed in the attempt, and the sobs burst out in almost convulsive rebellion against the effort to repress them. I put my arm round the neck of the poor young thing, and stooping down kissed her wet cheek, as a tear from my own eye mingled with her profuse weeping. The evidence of feeling appeared to overpower her utterly; she buried her head in my lap, and lay there long, sobbing like an infant. When the acuteness of the emotion had somewhat spent itself, I gently raised her up, and asked of her what was the cause of a grief so poignant. I found that I was now at last inside the intrenchments of her reserve; with a deep sigh she said, in her Scottish accent, it was "a lang, lang story," but if I cared to hear it, she would tell it. So sitting there, we two together, in the dim twilight of the night-lamp, with the shattered corpse of the railway-porter lying there "streekit" decently before us, she told the following pathetic tale:—

"I am an Aberdeen girl by birth. My father was the foreman at a factory, a very stiff, dour man, but a gude father, and an upright, God-fearing man. When I was about eighteen, I fell acquainted with a railway guard, a winsome, manly lad as ever ye would wish to see. If ye had kent my Alick, ye wadna wonder at me for what I did. My father was a proud man, and he couldna bear that I should marry a man that he said wasna my equal in station; and in his firm, masterful way, he forbade Alick from coming about the house, and me from seeing him. It was a sair trial, and I dinna think ony father has a right to put doon his foot and mar the happiness of twa young folks in the way mine did. The struggle was a bitter ane, between a father's commands and the bidding of true luve, and at last, ae night coming hame from a friend's house, Alick and I forgathered again, and he swore he would not gang till I had promised I would marry him afore the week was out.

"I'll not trouble ye with lang details of the battle that I fought with mysel', and how in the end Alick conquered. We were married in the West Kirk the Sunday after, and we twa set up our simple housekeeping in a single room in a house by the back of the Infirmary. Oh, mem, we were happy young things! Alick was the fondest, kindest man ye could ever think of. Sometimes he wad take me a jaunt the length of Perth in the van with him, and point out the places of interest on the road as we went flashing by them. Then on the Sunday, when he was off duty, we used to take a walk out to the Torry lighthouse, or down by the auld brig o' Balgownie, and then hame to an hour's read of the Bible afore I put down the kebbuck and the bannocks. My father kept hard and unforgiving: they tellt me he had sworn an oath I should never darken his door again, and at times I felt very sairly the bitterness of his feeling toward me, as I was sitting up waiting for Alick's hame-coming when he was on the night turn; but then he wad come in with his blithe smile and cheery greeting, and every thought but joy at his presence wad flee away as if by magic. Some of the friends I had kent when a lassie at home still kept up the acquaintance, and we used sometimes to spend an evening at one of their houses. The New Year time came, and Alick and myself got an invitation to keep our New Year's Eve at the house of a decent, elderly couple that lived up near the Kitty Brewster Station — quiet, retired folk that had been in business and made enough to live comfortable on. It was Alick's night for the late mail train from Perth, but he would be at Market Street Station in time to get up among us to see the auld year out and the new ane in; and I was to spend the evening there and wait for his arrival.

"It was a very happy time. The old couple were as kind as kind could be, and their twa or three young folks keepit up the fun brisk and lively. I took a hand at the cairts and sang a lilt like the rest; but I was luiking for Alick's company to fill up my cup of happiness. The time wore on, and it was getting close to the hour at which he might be expectit. I kenna what ailed me, but I felt strangely uneasy and anxious for his coming. 'Here he is at last!' I said to myself, as my heart gave a jump at the sound of a foot on the gravel walk. As it came closer, I kent it wasna Alick's step, and a strange, cauld grip of fear and doubt caught me at the heart. Mr. Thomson —

that was the name of our old friend — was called out, and I overheard the sound of a whispered conversation in the passage. Then he put his head in and called out his wife; I could see his face was as white as a sheet, and his voice shook in spite of himself. The boding of misfortune came upon me with a force it was in vain to strive against, and I rose up and went out into the passage amang them. The old man was shakin' like an aspen leaf; the gudewife had her apron ower her face, and was greetin' like a bairn, and in the door stood Tam Farquharson, a railway-porter frae the station. I saw it aa' quicker than I can tell it to you, leddy. I steppit up to Tam and charged him simple and straight.

"'Tom, what's happent to my Alick?'

"The wet tears stood in Tam's e'en as he answered, 'Dinna speer, Lizzie, my puir lass, dinna speer, whan the answer maun be a waefu' ane.'

"'Tell me the warst, Tam,' says I; 'let me hear the warst, an' put me 'oot o' my pain!'

"The words are dirlin' and stoonin' in my ears yet : —

"'The engine gaed ower him, and he's lyin' dead at Market Street.'

"I didna faint, and I couldna greet. Something gied a crack inside my head, and my e'en swam for a minute; but the next I was putting on my bonnet and shawl and saying good nicht to Mrs. Thomson. They tried to stop me. I heard Tam whisper to the auld man, 'She maunna see him. He is mangled oot o' the shape o' man.'

"But I was na to be gainsaid, and Tam took my airm as we gaed doon through the toon to Market

Street. There they tried hard to keep him oot frae my sight. They tellt me he was na fit to be seen, but there's nae law that can keep a wife frae seeing her husband's corpse. He was lying in a waiting-room covered up with a sheet, and, oh me! he was sair, sair mangled — that puir fellow there is naething to him — but the winsome, manly face, with the sweet familiar smile on it, was nane spoiled; and lang, lang, I sat there, us twa alane, with my hand on his cauld forehead, playing wi' his bonnie waving hair. They left me there, in their considerate kindliness, till the cauld light o' the New Year's morning began to break, and then they came and tellt me I must go. But I wadna gang my lane. He was mine, and mine only, sae lang as he was above the moulds; and I claimed my dead hame wi' me, to that house he had left sae brisk and sprightly when he kissed me in the morning. Four of the railway-porters carried him up to that hame which had lost its hame look for me now. . I keepit him to mysel' till they took him awa' frae me, and laid him under a saugh-tree in the Spittal Kirkyard."

She paused in her story, overcome by the bitter memory of the past, and I wanted no formal application now to give me the clew to her strange preference for the accident ward, and her hitherto inexplicable fondness for "railway cases." Poor thing, with what inexpressible vividness must the circumstances in which this New Year's night was passing with her, have recalled the sad remembrances of that other New Year's night, the narrative of which she had just given me! Presently she recovered her voice, and briefly concluded the little history.

"Leddy, I was wi' bairn when my Alick was taken

from me. Oh, how I used to pray that God would be good to me, and give me a living keepsake of my dead husband! I troubled nobody. I never speered if my father would do any thing for me; but I got work at the factory, and I lived in prayerful hope. My hour of trouble came, and a fatherless laddie was born into this weary world, the very picture of him that was sleeping under the tree in the Spittal Kirkyard. I needna tell ye I christened him Alick, and the bairn has been my joy and comfort ever since God gifted me with him. I found the sights and memories of Aberdeen too much for me, so I came up to London here, and ye ken the rest about me. It was because of being with my bairn that I wouldna agree to live in the hospital here like the rest of the nurses, and when I go home now to my little garret, he will waken up out of his saft sleep, rosy and fresh, and hold up his bonnie mou', sae like his father's, for 'mammie's kiss.'"

A HILL STORY.

It was not a very enlivening spot, lying as it did on the bleak lower shoulder of a lumpy hill, just where the heather merges into the coarse tufty grass which marks the margin of cultivation; yet it bore tokens of having at some time or other been a not discreditable homestead. I thought at first that it was the site of some old Roman camp; but a closer inspection dispelled the idea. There were the remains of the rough turf dike which once surrounded a kale-yard, and inside the grass was shorter and greener, while here and there among it a neglected southernwood or gooseberry-bush reared its ragged head, like the unkempt poll of some homeless street Arab. In one corner, overhung by a graceful but decaying weeping-willow, was a little plot which it required no conjurer to tell had been a flower-garden. The tortuous walks were still faintly defined by the straggling box edgings, with many a gap and many a withered stem, and through the luxuriant wilderness of chickweed, groundsel, and tansies, there peered forth an occasional cowslip and polyanthus, or a heart's-ease in its wretched forlornness belying its name. There was a gap in the turf wall just under the willow-tree, and passing out by it, I entered what had once been a trimly-kept back yard. The well was there, with its rough stone coping mouldering and displaced; at one time there had been a humble but not unambitious attempt to imitate an inlaid pavement with variegated pebbles laid down in some fantastic pattern; but the round stones had in some places been displaced from their bed, and in others a layer of mould coated them, out of which the rank strong grass grew with the fetid luxuriance of churchyard verdure. A pile of stone mixed with and matted together by turfs, or, as they are called in Scotland, divots, marked the site of the dwelling-house, of which what we had hitherto seen had been the adjuncts. Only a fragment of one gable still maintained its upright position, from the centre of which about half way up, projected the iron support for the crook, a few links of which still dangled as in mockery over the empty and green-moulded fire-stance. The whole scene wore an aspect of the forlornest desolation; not the faintest sign of human life was visible. The spring wind soughed through the quivering leaves of the willow, and played as if in mockery with a few fragments of paper, which, like the perturbed spirit, could find no rest anywhere — not a friendly crevice to drop into and moulder into pulp; but seemed condemned to be tossed to and fro on the wind eternally, as if they were the embodiment of some sinful human soul to which rest and peace were denied. One of these fragments I chased, and after a tussle with the wind-demon managed to possess myself of. It was the fly-leaf of a pocket Bible, and on it were written the two names —

"Isobel Crombie,
John Farquharson,"

and the legend underneath —

"Hereby plight constancy one to the other."

"Ah, said my friend and companion the old minister when I showed him the writing on the scrap I had picked up, "that is the key-note to a long and sad tale. My heart is always heavy when I come up out of the valley among these memorials of a once happy family. A parish minister sees much joy and much more sorrow in the course of what the busy world might call an uneventful life; but the story of these ruins is the saddest one within my experience."

I pressed the white-haired old man to tell me the tale. For a while he refused, urging that the subject was one which awakened sad memories, over which he would fain draw the curtain of oblivion; but at length he yielded reluctantly to my importunity. We seated ourselves on a fragment of the turf garden wall, and the old minister, after a short silence, occupied in the assiduous consumption of huge pinches of snuff, which perhaps accounted for a certain moisture of the eyes, and a somewhat profuse use of his pocket-handkerchief, began his story:—

"I was returning one winter's night from holding a catechising in a remote district of my parish, which lies at the back of the hill there. Poor old Jessie, my pony, had fallen lame on the way, and I turned off the hill-road up to the house, the ruins of which are now before us, to leave her there for the night. When I entered the kitchen, the cold ingle of which you see in that still standing gable, a very pleasant domestic scene met my eye. The gudeman was sitting in the lum-corner, reading aloud in a quaint effective way one of the hill stories of the Ettrick Shepherd. James Crombie, or 'honest James,' which was the name he was known by far and wide, was one of my oldest and most respected elders. He was a man somewhat of the old Cameronian type, with strongly-marked harsh features, a kindly gray eye, and a great pile of bald head, surmounted invariably by the 'braid bonnet' of the Scottish peasantry. The gudewife sat by the table opposite to her 'man,' listening to his reading with interest, and knitting away at a pair of 'furr and rigg' stockings for his sturdy shins. At the foot of the table sat their daughter Isobel, or Bell, as she was usually called, a bonnie sonsie lassie as there was in the parish. I had christened her myself (as indeed I had married her father and mother), and there was not a girl in the parish who had done better at the school, or on whom I could depend more implicitly for sensible answers at the half-yearly district catechisings I was wont to hold. By her side sat a strapping young fellow, John Farquharson by name, the son of a neighboring farmer, who was serving as ploughman to his father, and very soon expected, as I had been told, to get his name in the lease along with him. It was easy enough to see — by the way Bell blushed and John looked 'blate' as I came in — that there was a quiet courting-match going on between the young couple; and as the gudewife wore a complacent smile, with a sigh now and then as, perhaps, she thought of her own young days — and honest James certainly did not frown — I set down the whole little matter in my own mind as settled, and jocularly asked John when he was coming down to the manse to speak about the banns. He, of course, looked as if he had been detected in the act of stealing the pulpit

Bible, and Miss Bell gave me a half deprecatory, half malicious glance out of the corner of her bright blue eye, which I accepted on the spot as a tacit pledge that I was to perform the ceremony at a convenient season. After sitting with the group some twenty minutes, the gudeman insisted that I should conduct the evening family worship; and this over, I set out for the manse, accompanied by John Farquharson, because, as he said, 'the road was gey and kittle, and I micht layer in some o' the bog holes.'

"Time wore on. It was getting near to Midsummer, the season of the annual Commission Sacrament. The spring had been a very bad one; all the potatoes had gone wrong. Last year's crops had thrashed out wretchedly. A pestilence called the 'quarter ill' had smitten many of the cattle, and, in particular, James Crombie's byres had been almost emptied. His face had become perceptibly thinner and more haggard, and I used to meet him often stalking moodily along with his hands under his coat-tails, and his head sunk down on his breast. The young laird had come home from Oxford — a handsome, wild young scapegrace, about whom some ugly stories were already afloat. John Farquharson's face was no longer blithe and gay as it had been wont to be. The few times I had met him lately he seemed sullen and moody, and I feared something had intervened to prevent the course of true love running smooth between him and Bell. As for her, she, too, was altered. She had not come at all to the last catechising, and I had noticed her at church dressed in a way which hardly became her station.

"The sacrament time came, and James Crombie,

moody and careworn, was in his place with the other elders. The preliminary sermon had been preached, the sacred elements were on the white cloth which ran along the whole space of the middle of the church, and I ascended the pulpit to perform the awe-inspiring and terrible duty of 'fencing the tables.' Perhaps you know not the strict meaning of the phrase and the duty. It is this. With the Saviour's body and blood in a symbolical form before the minister and the intending communicants, it is the momentous task of the former to warn away from these tables, as he would from the very mouth of hell itself, all who would partake thereof with the flush of unrepented sin on their guilty souls. It is his dreadful duty to lift up his stern voice, and, in the name of the Most High, solemnly to tell 'the fornicators, idolaters, adulterers, effeminate, thieves, covetous, drunkards, revilers, extortionists, those full of envy, murder, deceit, malignity, backbiters, haters of God, despiteful, proud, boasters, inventors of evil things, disobedient to parents, without understanding, covenant-breakers, implacable, unmerciful' — to tell such, I say, in the name of the Master that, if they come to that table in their sins, they commit 'the sin against the Holy Ghost,' and incur the fate of the apostate Iscariot.

"This duty is, as I have said, a dread one; but it is not for the conscientious minister to shrink from it in all its awful significance. I was finishing the solemn sentences wherewith I 'fenced the tables,' when there was a sudden stir in the body of the church below me. I saw my favorite elder, James Crombie, spring to his feet, and, bareheaded, rush frantically out of the church, his 'lyart haffits' streaming behind him as he fled. It was only with an extraordinary effort that I controlled my emotion and was able to proceed; and when I saw the sensation the occurrence caused among the congregation — heightened when James's wife rose from her seat in the gallery, and, with white face and tottering steps, followed her husband — I wavered whether it would not be advisable to postpone the ordinance altogether. But I judged it better not; and table after table was served, and the afternoon sermon began in the church and the kirkyard ere I ventured to commune with myself over the extraordinary occurrence of the forenoon. I tried to connect it in some curious rambling fashion with the absence of the daughter, Isobel, from her usual seat in church; but, failing in this, the moment the benediction had been pronounced, I deputed a brother minister to fill my place at the manse table, and walked up the shoulder of the hill to James Crombie's house. A neighbor opened the door to me, and silently led the way into the kitchen. There, in her accustomed seat, sat the gudewife; but oh, how changed from the last time I had seen her there. She sat supine and motionless, as if she had been smitten with a palsy stroke, nor was she to be roused from out the deadly numbness into which she had been struck. There were no tidings of James, but the neighbor-woman pointed silently to an open letter which lay on the table. I took it up and read it. It ran thus, commencing with the stereotyped epistolary phraseology of the Scottish peasantry:

"'*Sunday Forenoon.*

"'DEAR MOTHER, — I write these few lines to let you know that I have gone away with young Mr. Harry, who has promised to marry me whenever we get to parts abroad. Dear

Father and Mother, do not fret, for I will come home soon, and be the leddy down at the big house. Tell John Farquharson he will get a better wife than your dutiful daughter till death,
            Isobel Crombie.'

"My heart turned sick; and after an ineffectual effort to rouse the old woman from her lethargy of woe, I left the grief-smitten house. On my way home I met John Farquharson coming toward me with rapid strides, and a wild, dangerous light in his eye. He had heard a rumor, and was coming to receive confirmation or refutation. I arrested his further progress, and strove, while I did not withhold from him the truth, to soften its terrible significance; but the moment he had gathered from me the confirmation of the report he had heard, he broke away with a bitter curse and a blood-curdling laugh, and ran madly across the moor as if flying from himself. There were heavy hearts that night in the manse, as well as up on the hillside.

"Next morning came tidings of James himself. He had walked straight, bonnetless as he was, from the church door to the gate of the jail in the county town, and commenced thundering at the door as if he meant to drive it in. The warder looked through the wicket, and, knowing James, asked, in surprise at the wildness of his appearance, what he wanted.

"'I want in,' was the answer, 'an' I maun be in. Gin ye dinna lat me in, I'll loup aff the pier-head, an' my bluid will be on yer head.'

"'Is the man mad?' was the warder's reply. 'Troth there's mony want oot here, but few want in. I tell ye gae awa', man!'

"'Let me in, I say,' was the response; 'pit me in a

cell, or I'll ding out my brains on the lintel o' the yett. I tell ye I've guilt on my soul, an' I maun dree the law for it.'

"The astonished official knew not what to make of so unprecedented a demand, and determined to get out of the responsibility of the matter by bringing James under the cognizance of the Procurator Fiscal, who lived in the next street. For his part, James was nothing loath, his whole being seeming to be centred in a feverish craving to be inside a felon's cell ere an hour was over. At the fiscal's he made a clean breast of it. Impelled, he said, by inability to pay his rent staring him in the face, he had signed the name of a neighbor on the back of a bill which he had handed to the factor in discharge of a portion of the rent due for his farm. Yes, 'honest James' was honest no longer — he was a forger and a felon. He had fallen, indeed, but he could not sear his conscience; and when my awful message, in fencing the tables, sounded in his ear, the burden of his secret sin had been greater than he could bear.

"The Procurator Fiscal of course took his deposition, and equally as a matter of course committed him to custody on the charge of forgery on his own confession. It was my task to tell the tale to his wife, and I would rather not trust myself to narrate the incidence of the grievous blow. The morning after my interview with her she was outside the prison door, and before the week was out there was a displenish sale at the steading among whose ruins we are seated. All James's debts were paid, and the poor gudewife removed into the town into a humble lodging, to be near her husband on the day of trial.

"That day was not long of coming. The Lords of Circuit entered the town at night, and next morning the Court was duly constituted. James Crombie's was the first case on the circuit roll. You must understand that whereas, were this case to have occurred in England, the factor, a private individual, would have been the prosecutor, and might have withdrawn from the charge had he thought proper, the law is different among us in Scotland here. The moment the Procurator Fiscal, who is a Crown official and the public prosecutor, has heard a whisper of the case, from that moment it is beyond the pale of private inveteracy or mercy, as the case may be; and if he, in the exercise of his judgment, reports to his superiors that it is one on which there is a reasonable probability of obtaining a conviction, no influence in the land can withhold it from the impartial arbitrament of the law. So, notwithstanding that the factor's claim had been satisfied, and that he had volunteered to give evidence as to character for the defence, which example had been imitated by the man whose name had been forged, James Crombie stood in the panel of the circuit courthouse to answer the charge, with a Crown counsel as prosecutor. As he stood in the dock with downcast eyes and worn face, I noticed that the sparse gray hairs had turned snow white, and the once stout upright figure had become wasted and bent.

"'How say you, James Crombie, are you guilty or not guilty?'

"His head sank still lower on his breast as the answer, although little louder than a whisper, sounded all over the hushed court, 'Guilty, my lord, before my God and before my fellow-man!'

"'The daumed feel,' I heard the Fiscal's clerk mutter angrily; 'an' me drew the process loose eneuch to drive a coach an' sax through't, to gie honest James a chance.'

"'Have you any counsel?' asked the court.

"'Nane, my Lord, except a guilty conscience.'

"A whispered consultation ensued between the Fiscal and the Crown counsel, and the latter rising, requested that the court would proceed to take proofs of substantiation of the charge, negativing the panel's confession and plea of 'guilty,' and that it would be pleased to appoint some of the counsel present to conduct the defence of the undefended prisoner at the bar.

"A brisk young advocate, who had been glancing over the papers, sprang up at this hint, and volunteered his services, which the court accepted on behalf of the seemingly bewildered panel, and the first witness — the factor — was called. He had not entered the witness-box, when the dapper young advocate was on his legs.

"'My Lud,' said he, 'I rise to save the time of the court and my learned brother who appears on behalf of the Crown. I beg to call your lordship's attention to the irrelevancy of the libel. It contains no specification of the date or the proximate date of the uttering of the document alleged to be forged.'

"The Fiscal's clerk seemed inclined to give vent to a hurrah; the court looked at the Crown counsel, who looked at the Fiscal, who smiled at his clerk and then shook his head, and then the Crown counsel rose and announced that 'he deserted the diet against James Crombie,' or, in other words, that he abandoned the charge. The door of the panel (or as you would call it, the dock) was opened, and the dazed, semi-unconscious man was let out and given over to his faithful wife.

"Next Sunday James Crombie was in my church in his usual seat. After public worship the session met according to their wont, and James came and stood at the door of the pew which he had so often entered of right as a respected elder of the congregation. The elders and myself judged that, in the circumstances, he might be permitted to resign *simpliciter*, and so denude himself of the office he was no longer worthy to hold. But no. James insisted on drinking the bitter cup to the dregs. 'I have been letten off ae punishment, oh ye that I anee cud caa' brethren, but I maun dree this weird to the vera end.' He was immovable; so next Sabbath day a Presbytery meeting convened in the kirk yonder, and James Crombie was silently deposed from the office of the eldership in the face of the congregation. With his fine bare head bent meekly downward he went out from our midst, his faithful wife guiding his footsteps. Next week they sailed for America. The ship was lost in the Channel, and not a soul saved."

It was with difficulty that the old minister reached what I judged to be the conclusion of his sad story. He rose from the turf with something that sounded like a sob, and walked with hasty steps down the slope, through the rough grass, and among the whin bushes. I followed him at a short interval, unwilling to interrupt his meditations, and we walked on in this fashion till we came within a little distance of the churchyard wall. Here the minister halted and faced about. Waiting till I came up, he abruptly burst again into speech.

"It was several years after this when a woman came to the manse and told me I was wanted up at the steading on the shoulder of the hill. I must tell you that Crombie's farm had been amalgamated into a neighboring one, and that the buildings, the ruins of which you have been among, were never afterwards occupied. With some curiosity I went up the hill, and crossing the threshold, from which the door-posts had rotted away. I entered the familiar kitchen. At first I saw no sign of life. But a low moaning drew me toward the chimney corner. There all along on the floor, a huddled mass of strange, draggled, tawdry finery, lay a female form, face downwards. I stooped, raised the passive head, and turned it to the light. For a time I gazed on the lineaments, worn, wild, and yet beautiful as they were, without a glimmer of recognition; then as she opened her eyes, the awful conviction dawned upon me that in this poor wreck, this waif and stray of blighted womanhood, I was looking upon none other than Isobel Crombie; and I was right. She recognized me, seemingly, after a little time; for she began in a low, broken tone to repeat scraps of the Shorter Catechism, and the texts of Scripture on which I had been wont to question her at the Sabbath school and on my season visitations. Then her mood changed, and sitting up, with wild distorted face and arms brandished frantically about, she burst into a torrent of raving oaths and blasphemy, such as curdled my blood within my veins. This outburst of horrible language lasted for a few minutes, and then the mood seemed to change again, and she began rocking herself to and fro, as if she were dandling an infant, crooning, at the same time, a low lullaby song. Finally she sank backward in a state of syncope, and then I sent the woman who had fetched me for some of the neighbors, and we had her carried into the nearest house. There she lay some days, evidently dying fast. Hers was the old story — so old in the history of womanhood that I need not relate it to you. It was a curious coincidence that while she was lying there fading out of the world, a letter came to me from the chaplain of Scutari Hospital to inform me that Private John Farquharson of the Scots Greys, had died on —— day of —— in that hospital, of desperate wounds received in the battle of Balaclava. We spared the poor wretch this last drop in the cup she had poured herself out. Halt, or you will tread on her grave!"

THE END.

www.ingramcontent.com/pod-product-compliance
Lightning Source LLC
Chambersburg PA
CBHW021812230426
43669CB00008B/721